IN THE MOOD
MARGE'S STORY

KARLEEN STEVENS

Published by *Greg Stevens*

For all enquiries, email greg.stevens3@bigpond.com

First published in Australia in 2022,
on the 95th birthday of *Margery Stevens*

Text copyright © Karleen Stevens, 2022
The moral right of the author has been asserted

All rights reserved

Without limiting the rights under copyright
reserved above, no part of this publication may be
reproduced, stored in or introduced into a retrieval system,
or transmitted, in any form or by any means (electronic, mechanical,
photocopying, recording or otherwise), without the prior
written permission of both the copyright owner and
the above publisher of this book

Photographs © Marge Stevens, 2022.
The author and publisher have taken every care to ask
permission from photographers and individuals wherever possible.

Typeset and cover design by *Blendid Pty Ltd*.
Suite 76, 66 Victor Crescent, Narre Warren, VIC, 3805

Typeset in 11/16 pt Adobe Garamond Pro by Adobe Systems.

Cover illustration © Graeme Whittle, 2022

This edition printed through IngramSpark.

ISBN: 978-0-6454489-0-0

This book is dedicated to a lady
who's been known by
many names
to many people,
    but to me
      will always be
          my
              Nanna Lune

# IN THE MOOD
Marge's Story

IN THE MOOD

CHAPTER ONE

Made of Stronger Stuff

* * *

December, 1932. A small group of five-year-old girls waits excitedly to appear on stage for their first end of year school concert. They are wearing costumes of crepe paper, made carefully for them by their mothers, and they fidget nervously, awaiting the moment they will be called forward and hoping they will remember what they have to do. Their teacher is keeping a close eye, and every so often has to remind them to sit still, lest they tear their costumes or spill something and cause the colours to run. Out in the hall they can hear the polite applause of their parents, though each one secretly knows that the biggest cheer will be for them.

There is one little girl among them, however, who is more curious than the others, and not very good at sitting still or being quiet. When the teacher isn't looking she tiptoes off down the hall, beckoning her friends to come along with her – they follow obediently, eager for an adventure. Underneath the hall they discover a warren of disused rooms and cupboards perfect for exploring, though it's very cold and damp and they must be careful not to catch their pretty paper dresses on the uneven walls. They play until they hear their names being called from above, and head back up to take their places on the warm, bright stage.

By the evening, the child has developed a chill, and the next day it has grown to a fever. Several days later she is finally diagnosed with pneumonia, and she lies on her side in a hospital bed, her breath rattling as the fluid is drained from her lungs. The doctors aren't sure if she's going to make it, and her mother, father and sisters are waiting outside anxiously for news. After several days hovering between life and death, the child rallies and the doctors announce that she will survive. When she wakes, she becomes aware of a large plaster covering most of her back, and it feels a bit like a giant piece of sticky tape. In a few more days she's recovered enough strength to have guests, and soon after that she is to be found bouncing energetically on the bed, giggling at the ward sisters who are caught between disapproval of her behaviour and relief that the child has survived. She returns home to her family, and it isn't long before she is running around with her sisters again, as fit and well as if the illness had never happened.

* * *

These are the earliest memories of Margery Frances Stevens, the second daughter of Robert Henry Stevenson, of Maryborough, and Kathleen May Walker, of South Yarra. She was born in Brighton, Victoria on Sunday May 1, 1927, a cold but fine day at the end of a cold, dry autumn.

Her father Robert was the only child of Walter Stevenson and Georgina Knight of Maryborough in Victoria, where he was born on April 30, 1904. Sometime after that the family moved to Brighton where Walter bought and ran a shop, and Robert was sent to the local school. His father was a stern man and not overly affectionate towards his son, and so Robert's childhood was one of rules, manners and obedience, in which children did not speak unless given express permission to do so.

Robert was a handsome young man, not overly tall at 5 feet 8 inches but with long legs, broad shoulders and a long, oval face. He kept his dark hair cut short and he had a dark complexion with grey eyes, a long, straight nose, heavy eyebrows and prominent ears. He was man of few words, perhaps as a result of his solitary upbringing, but when he did speak he made sure he was understood. After leaving school in his mid-teens he stayed in Brighton, where he took a job as an assistant in his father's shop.

Kathleen was his opposite in many ways. Born in South Yarra on March 19, 1905, she was a short woman – not much taller than five feet – with short, curly hair, a round face and chin and a button nose. She was the second of five children of Stephen Frederick Walker and Annie May Perkins, and her childhood was a busy and happy one, surrounded by chattering siblings and never lacking in parental affection. They settled in Brighton sometime after 1911, where Stephen found work as a butcher. Annie must have had a good repertoire of recipes to make the leftover cuts stretch between seven mouths, because Kathleen picked up on all her tricks and would go on to become a wonderful family cook herself.

Robert and Kathleen met in high school and were married in Brighton on May 9, 1925, when Robert was 21 and Kathleen was 20. Sadly, neither of their mothers was there to see it, as Georgina had died in 1923 at the age of 44, and Annie in 1922 at only 41. Their first daughter was born 11 months later, on April 9, 1926, and they called her Yvonne, a foreign name which Robert could never get used to. He called her Bonny instead, because she was such a bonny lass, and the name stuck – she would be known as Bonny her entire life. Marge was born 13 months later, and another sister, Shirley, arrived 15 months after that in August 1928. A fourth daughter, Norma, followed in November of 1929. They were a close-knit family, and Marge's early years were spent primarily in the company of her sisters and her parents.

Sometime in those first few years the family moved to Paddington in

Sydney, where Robert took a job as a hod carrier in the construction industry. A hod was a three-sided metal box attached to a long pole, used for carrying bricks. The hod carrier would hoist the hod over his shoulder and carry the bricks – up to 10 or 12 at a time – from the pallets to the bricklayers, wherever they were on the site, which often meant going up and down ladders. He might also have helped with mixing and carrying the mortar, and it would have been his responsibility to ensure that the bricks and the mortar were delivered at the correct rate for the bricklayers to work continuously.

It was around this time that the Great Depression hit, and unemployment in Australia rose to 30% in some places. Many families were moving from cities out to the country, where some were forced to work for low or no pay in return for housing and space to grow vegetables. Fortunately for Robert, there was plenty of work in construction and he was able to keep his job. He was a builder by nature, always fixing and tinkering with his bike and other people's cars, and eventually when Robert and Kathleen bought a block of land outside Bankstown, he built their house himself. Bankstown was a small town then, with a church, post office and a small corner store opposite the school. The Stevensons' house sat in a large paddock a mile or two out of town, surrounded by bush on all sides, and to four small girls it seemed like they had all the space in the world to themselves. They had two bedrooms – one for Robert and Kathleen and one for the girls – and Marge shared a double bed with her sister Bonny, which was a normal arrangement in the days before central heating and electric blankets. There was a large kitchen which doubled as a dining and family room, with a wood stove at one end and a large table where they sat for meals. At the other end was a small sitting area, where two easy chairs sat opposite an open fire. Eventually, after several years of persistent requests from Kathleen, Robert built a laundry at the back, and their humble country home was complete.

In March 1931 the family grew from six to seven with the birth of Marge's brother Frederick. Robert and Kathleen were thrilled to finally have a boy in the family, and his sisters were delighted to have a baby brother to dote upon – not to mention a real-life baby for their games of make-believe. He was the apple of his parents' eye, and although his sisters always insisted that he was spoiled, they loved him very much too.

In May 1932 Marge turned five, and it was time for her to start school. She was scared to go at first, and didn't want to leave Kathleen, but she went along with her sister Bonny and it wasn't long before she learned to enjoy it. If there was anything that scared her, or she thought she couldn't do, her mother simply pointed out, in her most matter-of-fact voice, 'there's no such thing as can't, at least not until you try'. Her sister Shirley started school the year after Marge, and Norma the year after that, so in a small school of about 60 or 70 students where there were usually several ages in one class she always had one or more of her sisters with her. The four of them walked there and back together each day, enjoying the freedom and the carefree time in each other's company.

It was around this time that she caught pneumonia, after an end of year concert at school, and she was admitted to the Northshore Hospital for Infectious Diseases in St Leonards, north of Sydney. It had taken several days for doctors to diagnose her condition, so by the time she was admitted to hospital she was dangerously unwell. This was in the days before penicillin, but a new antibiotic serum, sulphapyridine, had recently been introduced and had significantly lowered the mortality rate of the disease – on the other hand, Marge was very young and the disease was significantly advanced, and the doctors did not expect her to survive.

She was obviously made of stronger stuff than they imagined, however, because she made a full recovery and returned to school in the new year. Her lessons in the 1930s included reading, writing and spelling, arithmetic, drawing, and a little bit of world history, and Marge was an eager student. She and her classmates sat in pairs at small wooden desks, each with their own pens and ink bottles, while the teacher stood at the front with her blackboard and chalk. Every day they practiced writing on special paper with lined pages underneath, using blotting paper to dry it afterwards. It took practice not to splat or spill the ink, and there were many failed attempts, and many reprimands, before she got the hang of it, and as if the ink wasn't enough to contend with, there were also troublesome boys who were always on the lookout for mischief. Anyone unlucky enough to be sitting next to one often went home with ink flicked on their clothes, which got them into even more trouble with Kathleen.

Punishment in those days was sparse but harsh and mostly administered to students who spoke out of turn or made mistakes. In those days, the teacher's word was law and children were expected to listen and obey. Any challenges or impertinent questions were answered with a slap – also known as a cut – across the back of the hand from a strap or a ruler. Incorrect spelling, errors in arithmetic or writing outside the lines were offences all serious enough to earn a cut, but more serious offences, such as fighting in the playground, warranted a few lashings of the strap across the bottom. Fortunately, Marge was a well-behaved student and wasn't in trouble very often, but she did suffer several cuts over the years for talking and for incorrect spelling – something the teacher did not trouble to help her with, despite the fact that she always found it difficult. Individual attention was not a feature of schooling in the 1930s, and if a child didn't understand something they simply had to get on as best they could and hope to avoid the notice of the teacher and her strap.

During breaks the children played out in the yard where they had swings, balls and skipping ropes. Sometimes when they had bread and butter Marge and her sisters picked nasturtium leaves and made them

Chapter One – Made of stronger stuff

into a sandwich, savouring the peppery taste. They were each given a bottle of milk to drink every day, provided by the state government and delivered to the school in great rattling crates. It was usually warm and tasted horrible by the time it reached the children, but they were not given any choice about whether to drink it or not. This provided essential extra nourishment for the ones who may not have been getting enough at home, but for the Stevenson children – who were always well fed by Kathleen – it was an ordeal that would put them off drinking milk for the rest of their lives.

When they weren't at school, Marge and her sisters filled their days playing outside in the empty paddock next to their house. They didn't have many toys, so they entertained themselves with games of make-believe and dressing up in clothes their mother gave them. They had a few books which they sometimes read in the evenings or in bad weather, but they were more often to be found outside, enjoying their games in the shade of the wattle trees that grew alongside the paddock fence.

They were generally well-behaved, and their mother trusted them to stay close and come in at the right time. But even though they didn't intend to be naughty, sometimes it happened anyway, with alarming results. There came a day, when Marge was about ten or eleven, when their mother had to go into town by train, and as she was not familiar with the walk to the station the children, who walked that way to school every day, escorted her there. The route crossed several paddocks and involved climbing through or over various gates and fences, and as Kathleen was not likely to remember it, the children promised to be back later to meet her off the return train. While they had some time to themselves at home, the children decided to treat themselves to a party. Carefully and meticulously, they set the table with all of Kathleen's precious crystal glasses and imagined they were having a splendid time of dinner and drinks, completely forgetting, of course, that they were supposed to go and collect their mother. Hours later, in she walked looking tattered and dishevelled, having got completely lost crossing the fields to get back home. It was one of only a few times they were severely scolded by their mother, who neglected to notice or acknowledge that at least none of the crystal glasses had been broken.

On another occasion it was Freddie who bore the brunt of his sisters' inattention. Being the smallest – and significantly outnumbered – put him at a disadvantage, especially when it came to playing games and tricks. He was usually bullied into playing the smallest role in any game of make-believe, and was in no position to resist, or to do anything about it, if he didn't want to. For example, one day he and the girls were playing a game of Cowboys and Indians and Freddie was cast as the unfortunate captive, being the easiest to tie to a post. When the call came for tea, the girls ran inside and left him there, strapped to a post out in the middle of the field. They were scolded, of course, and though Freddie came to no harm, he remained indignant about the episode for a long time afterwards.

Life in Bankstown settled into a pattern. In the 1930s the first breakfast cereals were becoming available, so in the mornings after getting up and dressed the children enjoyed Weet-Bix or Rice Bubbles before school. Kathleen packed them each a sandwich with a piece of fruit and home-made cake, then they walked together from their home on Miller Road, across the paddock, up a dirt road and across a main road to Bass Hill. It took them about half an hour – longer if they stopped to look at things, which they often did. In those days it was always considered safe to walk, and they knew not to talk to strangers.

They made the journey there and back every day, whatever the weather, always careful to stick together, and in the evenings Kathleen always had a meal prepared for them. Money was tight, and with seven mouths to feed she learned to make food go a long way. She cooked everything on the wood stove, mostly simple food designed to fill up a hungry family, including some new recipes that were appearing at the time like shepherd's pie and Irish stew. Roasts were a Sunday staple, but Kathleen's speciality was stew with dumplings, which she cooked for exactly 20 minutes without taking the lid off, so they always came out perfectly. There were always home-grown vegetables, which ensured a ready supply of potatoes, carrots and onions, and depending on the season there might also be pumpkins, cabbage, cauliflower, turnips, swedes, celery, sweet potato or garlic. For dessert, rice puddings were common – being the most filling – or for a special treat it might be sponge pudding and cream. By this time cocoa, custard powder and desiccated coconut were cupboard staples, so lamingtons, Anzac biscuits, melting moments and chocolate crackles became a standard part of the Australian mother's baking arsenal. Despite all this, Kathleen was most proficient at making cakes, which she whipped with her hands, because she said it made them lighter.

There was no refrigeration in those days. Instead, they had an old Coolgardie food safe, which was a rickety storage box with a wooden frame surrounded by wire mesh and a tray on the top to hold water. Hessian, or another type of fabric such as flannel, would be placed in the water tray so that most of it was hanging down over the sides of the box, and the whole thing was placed in an exposed area so a breeze could pass through, cooling the contents inside. Meat wrapped in calico could be stored in this way for about 24 hours, so it was important to only purchase and use what they needed each day – they couldn't afford to waste anything.

Money may have been tight and the girls and Freddie may not have had many luxuries, but they never went hungry. Milk was delivered each morning, and the butcher and greengrocer called regularly to deliver meat and groceries such as bread, butter, sugar and eggs. It was all packaged up in a tidy paper bag, and occasionally there might be a tin of biscuits as a special treat. Whenever she made a roast, Kathleen kept the dripping to have with bread, and sometimes they had bread with jam – butter was saved for cooking, or for bread and butter pudding. Kathleen had no means of transport and could not go into town very much, so if she needed anything else Robert picked it up after work and brought it home on his motorbike.

Despite being very much appreciated, family dinners were not social occasions. Robert was a stern man, having been raised an only child by a stern father, and as a father in turn he was aloof and distant. Though the children looked up to him, they feared his temper as well. He was not affectionate with them, nor was he one to comfort or console them in their troubles, preferring to leaving those duties to his wife. His role was one of providing means and discipline, and he expected his children to be well-behaved at all times. As a child, he had never been allowed to speak at the dinner table, and he demanded the same standard from his own children. Sitting in silence, however, was not a strong point for Marge, as she was a very social and interactive person even in those days, so she was often scolded for speaking at the table and sent to her room with no dinner. Her mother, never lacking in affection or care, always made sure to bring her up something to eat afterwards, a display of tenderness which Marge never forgot.

Sometimes in the evenings Robert attended meetings of the Labour party at the local hall, which every working man did then, and occasionally he and Kathleen went to a ball, but most evenings after dinner would find them sitting in the easy chairs by the fire, reading the newspaper or listening to the wireless while they sipped a cup of tea. There was no coffee available then, only chicory, but the children sometimes enjoyed a hot cocoa. Those that hadn't been sent up to bed could do their homework or perhaps help Kathleen with the sewing. This was always tricky for Marge, who tried learning to use her mother's old treadle machine but couldn't get the hang of the pedal and could never get her hands and feet to work at the same time. Kathleen tried to teach her crochet, but no matter how many times Kathleen reminded her 'there's no such thing as can't', like sewing it was not for her. In a stroke of initiative, she borrowed two wooden meat skewers from the butcher and taught herself to knit, and so from then on her evenings became occupied with the clicking of knitting needles and the production of simple but useful items like scarves, hats and tea cosies.

On weekends the children were expected to help their mother around the house, and Marge, who didn't like cooking, usually volunteered to do the polishing and sweeping. On Sunday mornings the whole family attended the service at the local Methodist church, where the children all attended Sunday School. They each had their own bible, and each week they were given a stamp to stick in the front to mark their attendance. Marge always enjoyed the lessons and stories, especially when they sat outside, and she loved to join in singing songs with the other children.

Every couple of months they went together to the markets in Sydney, where Robert and Kathleen shopped for supplies they couldn't get from the grocer or corner store, such as hats and shoes for themselves and the children. As a special treat, they bought the children meat pies with peas (known as a pie floater now) and sometimes an ice cream as well. Kathleen also bought material, often choosing ends or bundles to save money, which she used to make all their clothes. With four girls, most of the clothes were handed down from one to another, but Freddie as the only boy had to have his shirts and shorts made from scratch. Robert always needed extra clothes for work, as they often came back more dirty and dusty than the children's, as well as one good suit for church and meetings. Kathleen washed them all in the old copper, which was a large metal boiler with space for a fire underneath to heat the water. Once clean, they were wrung through a wooden mangle and hung out to dry, then pressed with a flat iron that she heated on the stove. Once a week Kathleen used the copper to boil water for the bath, and the children took turns to jump in and have a wash. There was always a scramble to get in as early as possible, since the water became colder and dirtier with each occupant. It was a laborious operation, especially for Kathleen, and having a bath once a week was considered perfectly adequate in those days.

One year Robert bought an old T-model Ford, and each summer following that the family went on holiday to Port Stephens, about three hours up the coast from Sydney at the mouth of Tillgerry Creek. All seven of them piled in, the four girls squeezed into the back with Freddie sitting on someone's knee, and off they'd go for a few days relaxing and playing on the beach. They built sand castles, slurped ice creams and played in rock pools, but if they wandered too far into the creek they ended up covered in leeches, which made the girls all scream and come running out in a great panic. These were happy times, rare occasions when Marge could see her parents relax. She never learnt to swim, but she loved the water nonetheless, so different as it was to the bush they were used to. She was the fairest of her sisters, with auburn hair and pale skin like her mother, and she was always getting sunburnt – fortunately Kathleen always had a slice of tomato or cucumber to cool it down.

In winters more of Kathleen's remedies became necessary with the onset of colds and flus. Marge was always the most sickly – the bout of pneumonia she'd survived as a small child had taken its toll – so every day during the cold months her mother made her an egg flip, which a glass of milk with a raw egg and maybe some vanilla to flavour it. Marge found it disgusting, but protests fell on deaf ears, and down it had to go. For sore throats, Kathleen acquired eucalyptus from a local farm and put a few drops on a spoonful of sugar for the children to swallow, and for infections she made a poultice of velvet soap and sugar. If a child was unlucky enough to get croup they were given an infusion of onions in vinegar, and whenever the children picked up hair lice she treated it with Quassia Chips, which was bark from a particular tree with anti-parasitic qualities. The chips had to soak in a bowl of water over night until the water turned brown, then it was warmed up and rinsed through the offending hair.

Occasionally the neighbours visited, which was a welcome break for Kathleen whose days were mostly filled at home cleaning and cooking on her own. There was one neighbour who was a contortionist and entertained them by squeezing herself into the old copper, much to the delight and fascination of the children. There were also visits from various family members, in particular from Kathleen's sisters Nellie and Irene, who the children knew as Aunty Nell and Aunty Rene. Aunty Nell was very sophisticated and lived in Sydney with her husband and two boys. Once or twice Marge went to stay with her, but she found her cousins too rowdy and she missed her mother, so she didn't go if she could avoid it. There was a third aunt, Lillian, and an uncle on Kathleen's side too, her younger brother Robert, who the children never met. In fact, they didn't even learn of his existence until they were much older, as he had been born with a mental disability, and in those days these things were covered up and not talked about – especially not to children.* The same attitude applied to deceased relatives, and asking questions was not encouraged. As a result, Marge and her siblings grew up knowing very little about their grandmothers.

---

* Robert was born in 1907 and died in 1939, probably in the Aradale Lunatic Asylum in Ararat. It was closed in 1993 and is now a museum.

On the other hand, they often made trips to visit their grandfathers in Victoria, and they had to be on their best behaviour. Their Grandfather Walker – Kathleen's father Stephen – lived in Melbourne but Robert's father Walter – Grandfather Stevenson to the children – had returned to Maryborough after the death of his wife and had quite a large house with plenty of garden space. He was strict like their father, and he expected perfect table manners. The children had to sit still and not speak until they were spoken to, and woe betide any one of them if they so much as sniggered when he slurped his tea! They had no aunts and uncles on Robert's side, but Walter had four brothers and two sisters, so they had plenty of second cousins to get to know and to play with in the large space outside. Visits became even more interesting in 1936 when Walter remarried. His new wife, Janet, was the widow of his brother Fred, and she had no children of her own. She enjoyed their company almost as much as the nips of sherry she sipped on the side, and the children in turn found her most amusing. No doubt they were delighted to be let in on her little secret.

Back in Sydney, life went on in the usual routine of school, family visits and church, but occasionally there was a national event which brought some excitement and variety to their lives, and one of these was the celebration in 1938 of the 150th anniversary of the landing of the First Fleet in Sydney Harbour. Several months of events and ceremonies were planned in Sydney, starting with a day of celebrations on January 26. It was a morning of brilliant sunshine as over a million people – roughly two-thirds of the population – lined the streets for a pageant which began with a re-enactment of Captain Phillip's landing at Farm Cove in 1788. This was followed by a parade of floats depicting various aspects of Australian life, including an enormous teapot float emblazoned with the words 'Australia's National Drink'. The day finished with a dazzling display of fireworks and was declared a great success, despite record numbers of faintings and collapses which were attended by the local volunteer services.

Sydney Harbour was full of visiting warships, and the New South Wales Premier Sir Bertram Stevens received a message from the British Government congratulating the country on its sesquicentenary and paying tribute to "the far-sighted wisdom with which Sydney's first founders selected a spot at once so beautiful and so blessed with natural advantages". Even the Sydney Morning Herald joined in the rhetoric, relating scenes of jubilation lasting far into the night. After describing the crowds that had gathered in the city as appreciative, orderly and a model of good behaviour, it declared that:

> "...tired though they were, and even hungry, perhaps, the multitude which contributed to the success of this unique festival went to their homes convinced that they had seen a new vision of their country – a country generated from the small seed of a crown colony, now grown to the stature of a nation."

The nation was gripped by a mood of pride and nostalgia and the carnival atmosphere lasted for several months. School children had their own program of celebrations, and throughout March and April a calendar of events was planned for them that included a music festival in the Town Hall, another festival at the Sydney Cricket Ground and a swimming and athletics carnival. Because the initial celebrations took place in the school holidays they were able to attend the pageants and concerts, although one regional newspaper lamented the fact that they were not in school at the time, as the celebrations should possess the greatest interest for the young:

> "The rising generation should be impressed with the achievements of their ancestors. If they ask questions about the forced passengers of the first fleet, it will be well, because it can be explained to

> *them that it was not long before the transportation of convicts was discontinued, and, moreover, some of the convicts were sent overseas for what could be regarded as very trivial offences, such as poaching rabbits."*

The 150th Anniversary celebrations lasted until Anzac Day on April 25, and probably the biggest event – arranged deliberately to coincide with the celebrations – was the third Empire Games hosted in Sydney. For one week in February the nation was glued to its wirelesses as Australia played host to seven nations in twenty men's and eight women's track and field events. Nearly 40,000 people packed into the Sydney Cricket Ground for the opening ceremony, where the Australian flag bearer, cyclist Dunc Grey, read the Oath of Amateurism as 2,000 pigeons were released. The New South Wales Governor, Lord Wakehurst, then read a message from King George VI, which read:

> *"I shall be grateful if you will express to all participating in the British Empire Games my hearty thanks for their loyal assurances. I send my best wishes for the success of the Games, the results of which I shall follow with interest, and I am particularly glad to know that they have attracted to Sydney the representatives of so many parts of the Empire."*

The ceremony ended with a stirring rendition of *Rule Britannia* and within ten minutes the track events had started. Canada topped the medal tally with 8 Golds, but Australia came out on top overall with 29 out of a possible 84 medals. Decima Norton was the host nation's most successful athlete, winning five out of Australia's six gold medals and earning herself the nickname 'The White Streak'. The Sydney Morning Herald declared it "the most important athletic carnival ever held in Australia" – and in 1938, it was hard to argue with that.

In general, Marge had a happy childhood. She knew nothing but love and affection from her mother, who she was very close to. She respected her father, and though he was strict with her, she was too busy with school and play for it to bother her too much. She enjoyed learning and socialising with other children and particularly loved playing with her sisters and brother. Although she didn't have much in the way of possessions, there was always enough to eat, clothes to wear and games to play, which was plenty for her to be content. She may not have been the most ambitious child, but she had a knack for finding joy in any situation, and it was a trait that would serve her well in the changing times to come.

CHAPTER TWO

A Girl of Fair Ability

* * *

On the first day of September in 1939, Germany invaded Poland, setting off a chain of events which would change the world irrevocably. Two days later Great Britain, as it had warned it would, declared war on Germany, and Australia, as a dominion of the British Empire, was obliged to follow suit. The Prime Minister Sir Robert Menzies was notified of the decree, and the Governor General, the Honourable Alexander Hore-Ruthven, proclaimed that Australia was once again in a state of war.

It's not difficult to imagine, at this moment, Robert, Kathleen and their children sitting around the wireless in the large kitchen which doubled as a sitting room, listening to their prime minister declaring to the nation that they were once again following their mother country into battle, this time against the Nazi war machine:

> "If such a policy were allowed to go unchecked there could be no security in Europe and there could be no just peace for the world," he said to the nation. "A halt has been called. Force has had to be resorted to, to check the march of force. Honest dealing, the peaceful adjustment of differences, the rights of independent peoples to live their own lives, the honouring of international

obligations and promises, all these things are at stake. There never was any doubt as to where Great Britain stood in relation to them. There can be no doubt that where Great Britain stands, there stand the people of the entire British world."

He emphasised the fact that the war would require supplies and foodstuffs as much as soldiers, sailors and airmen, and urged the people to keep business and production going. He called for calmness, resoluteness, confidence and hard work in the bitter months to come, and called on their pride and patriotism in assisting with the war effort: "I know that in spite of the emotions we are all feeling, you will show that Australia is ready to see it through. May God in his mercy and compassion grant that the world may soon be delivered from this agony".

The world was changing forever, and even for a young girl in Sydney the effects could be felt. School continued in the same way, with a new addition to the curriculum: Air Raid Drills. By this time in Australia, Air Raid Precaution committees had been organised in each state, and emergency shelters were set up around the country. The drills therefore became part of the routine, and the children had to learn where their nearest shelter was. If they heard the sirens while they were at school they had to abandon their desks immediately and practise moving to their designated refuge.

Apart from the air raid drills, life in Bankstown carried on in much the same way, but there was another change to come: at the beginning of 1940 Marge started high school at the Bankstown Domestic Science School. High school was more formal than primary school, and now she had to wear a uniform: a pleated navy skirt and white blouse, with black shoes and white socks, and her long, fair hair was tied back by her mother in a ponytail or plait. It was an all-girls school, and under no circumstances were they to talk to the boys in the next school through gaps in the wire fence. The Headmistress, Miss Wheeler, was very strict and she expected her pupils to behave like ladies at all times. She would not tolerate any talking or fidgeting, which is something, we might assume, that Marge had extreme difficulty with.

There was more to learn now, and subjects increased to include dictation, English history, geography, botany and horticulture, domestic arts and sciences, and business. In her first six months of high school, Marge's results showed a similar pattern to her primary school studies: her arithmetic scores were good, but her English and history scores were low. She did well in her new subjects of geography, cookery and needlework, but her best marks by far were in business principles and bookkeeping where she earned scores of 77 and 80 respectively, compared to just 32 in English literature. She also struggled with sewing – failing, as she had before on her mother's machine, to get her hands and feet to work together between the pedal and the machine. As a result, all her sewing work had to be done by hand, which took much longer and unsurprisingly she didn't enjoy it. She was good at handwriting, though, now that she didn't have boys flicking ink on her, and one year did very well at the Bass Hill Mothers' Club Amateur Horticultural Show, winning second prize for Brushwork and first prize for Best Handwriting Under 14. She was kept busy, and though news of the war filtered down to her and her sisters, apart from the air raid drills – which continued in high school – its effect on her life was minimal and she gave it little thought.

Things changed, however, in the second half of 1940, shortly after the fall of France to the Germans. This prompted a surge of volunteers in Australia, and coincided with the Army raising its maximum recruiting age from 35 to 40 years – so at 36, Robert decided to enlist. At the time he was working as a lorry driver, and although wages were slowly increasing as Australia came out of the Depression, wages in the transport sector were still below the state average at 96 shillings and 3 pence a week.* As a private in the Australian Imperial Force he would be entitled to 5 shillings a day, plus another 3 shillings for being married and an extra allowance of 1 shilling per dependent child per day. That would be a total of 91 shillings a week – slightly less than he was earning before but it did include his room and board. He would send most of it home to Kathleen, who would have to learn to make do on the reduced wage, but at least there was one less mouth to feed.

On May 23 he presented himself at the Engineers' Drill Hall in Paddington, where he was declared fit for service and made his oath to serve his King and country. From now on, he would spend very little time with his family. He was sent for his compulsory three months training to Rosebery, an old racecourse in the southern suburbs of Sydney which had been converted into a training ground, and then to Ingleburn Army Camp. He was assigned to the 2/13th Battalion, which was made up primarily of volunteers from New South Wales and formed part of the second Australian Imperial Force (AIF) 20th Brigade.

At the beginning of August he spent four days sick in hospital, then rejoined his unit in Bathurst where they had their final collective training. On September 2 he was given his assignment as batman to the chaplain – a kind of valet or assistant to a priest or pastor. This was considered a desirable position, as batmen were generally handpicked by senior officers and often enjoyed extra pay and privileges. Robert's experience may have worked in his favour, and at his age he was unlikely to be promoted through the ranks, so he must have felt very fortunate to land the position. At the end of September he was granted a week's leave in which he came

---

*   Until February 1966, the Australian currency was based on the English system of pounds, shillings and pence, represented as £, s and d. One pound was worth twenty shillings, and one shilling worth twelve pence. Therefore, Robert's wages would be written as 96/3 or £4/16/3.

home to visit the family, before returning to camp on October 5. This was the last his family would see of him for some time, as on the 19th of that month he embarked with 7,000 men from Sydney on the Queen Mary as Private Stevenson, bound for the Middle East.

While Robert was completing his training, Marge carried on with high school with a definite drop in enthusiasm. In the second half of the year she improved slightly in history and home decoration, but most of her grades went down noticeably and she was still having trouble with her sewing and spelling. It's clear she was not enjoying school as much any more – by November her class had shrunk from 59 pupils to 45, and she was obviously keen to leave school and join the work force as many of her classmates, including her older sister Bonny, had done. At that time, however, the school leaving age in New South Wales was 14, and as Marge was only 13, there was nothing she could do. She had to carry on with her lessons, and so she started her second year of high school in January 1941.

That year brought still more changes for the family. Robert was now away at war, and since he was abroad the only news they had from him was by letter. Soldiers who sent most of their pay home to their wives were left with about one shilling per day, enough for their tobacco and one airmail stamp per week. For security reasons, he was not allowed to tell them where he was or reveal any details relating to their operations, and in fact, many of his letters had been redacted with parts blacked or cut out – something that must have been a source of great anxiety to Kathleen, but was one of great amusement to the children. Instead, perhaps he would have related stories about his work as a batman, or the chaplain he was assigned to – probably Chaplain Cyril Francis, who was assigned to the 2/13th and travelled with them on the Queen Mary. The term itself came from the old English word 'bat', meaning pack saddle, and so the primary duty of the batman would have been to look after and transport the officer's equipment – possibly by horse or mule, but it's possible by Robert's time that the chaplain had an army vehicle at his disposal, in which case Robert's experience as a lorry driver would have made him perfectly suited to the role. His work would also have included acting as a runner to convey messages to and from the chaplain, cleaning and polishing his uniform or acting as his personal bodyguard.

He might have told them about his journey to the Middle East aboard the Queen Mary, or perhaps of their stopover in Bombay, which for many of the men was their first encounter with a culture other than their own. They rested in a staging camp and were not allowed to go to the nearby village, although of course some men did, and the poverty and squalor were apparent even to men living cheek by jowl in a troopship. They continued their journey and arrived in El Kantara in Egypt on November 26 where they boarded land trains to Gaza Ridge in Palestine for further training. The training was hard, designed to toughen them up, and involved a lot of marching on the sand and assembling and disassembling Bren guns in hot and windy conditions. They lived in tents on a flat and dusty area near a small town, from which several inhabitants were hired as cleaners and interpreters. Soldiers weren't supposed to mix with the locals, but here they found that their meagre wages stretched a lot further than at home and many of them took advantage of the taxi services to get around the area. They were enthralled by the local souk, and bought souvenirs, coffee and meal cakes which they enjoyed hot off the grill. They were forbidden from buying fruit for fear of dysentery, but some of them did anyway and stall holders learnt to say 'very sweet, very hygienic' when plying their wares. They were still there for Christmas and many of them applied for two or three-day leave passes to visit Bethlehem and Jerusalem, while others went to Alexandria via the Suez Canal.

In February they were deployed to Benghazi in Libya, but were forced to withdraw soon afterwards when German forces landed in North Africa. They retreated to Tobruk, a port city near the Egyptian border, with the 2/13th forming the rear guard. The battalion fought a short battle at Er Regima on April 4, defending an 11 kilometre stretch of rocky high ground alongside a British artillery division, holding off 3,000 German soldiers long enough for the rest of the troops to reach safety. They nearly lost one of their chaplains, a Padre Salter, who had a keen interest in archaeology and was almost caught by the Germans when he stopped to collect some stone age tools that he found lying among the rocks and debris – fortunately his battalion persuaded him to come back another time. By late evening vehicles were sent to retrieve the defending troops and they were transferred to the safety of Tobruk. This action made the 2/13th the first Australian Army unit to see action against the Germans, but it cost them 98 soldiers – probably including friends and comrades of Robert's.

The battalion in Tobruk formed part of a 35,000 strong garrison of Allied troops, some 14,000 of which were AIF. A week after they arrived, on April 11, the port came under attack from the Afrika Corps of the German-Italian army, and they remained there under siege for most of the year, successfully holding off enemy troops. For the first few months, the 2/13th concentrated on building and consolidating the port's defences, using a pre-existing network of underground defensive positions built by the Italian army before the war. They were at a disadvantage, being far from any air support bases, and supplies had to be shipped in under cover of darkness to avoid being spotted by enemy fighters. Several supply ships were lost, but at least the Allies had the means to fight back, and with land-based missiles were able to take down a number of enemy bombers.

Conditions during the siege could be uncomfortable and dangerous. The trenches and tunnels were full of fleas and vermin and they were constantly filling up with sand. If they closed up the openings to stop the sand and insects getting in, they became stiflingly hot. The surrounding desert was littered with German booby traps – anything from thermos flasks, pens or even shaving sticks that had been rigged with explosives and left lying in the sand, disguised as litter in the shifting landscape. Sandstorms were a daily occurrence, outbreaks of dysentery were common and once their individual rations ran out there was nothing but tinned food to eat until a resupply ship could reach them through enemy lines. Discipline was strict and misdemeanours were punished with tedious but necessary tasks like polishing nails.

It wasn't all bad, though. Soldiers were rostered leisure time and tents were set aside for letter writing and games, and there were several Monopoly sets available. Robert wrote many letters home, and although he couldn't tell his family where he was or any information relating to military tactics, he might have told them about the tough conditions, of being surrounded by heat and dust and the incessant sound of sand trickling into the trenches. Perhaps he described his surroundings as he took in the blinding yellow sand, the dazzling blue of the Mediterranean or the unfamiliar constellations of the cold desert nights.

He might have written about his visit to the Australian General Hospital in June, where he spent eight days recovering from pyrexia before rejoining his unit on the 11th of that month.* He could have told them of his meals and rations, which – when the supply ships could get in – might have included corned beef in a tin, plain or sweet Arnott's biscuits, hard sweets or mints, tinned tuna or Weet-Bix, which could be eaten dry or boiled with water and sugar. If the men were lucky, they might even have been

---

* Pyrexia, also known as Trench Fever, was a term given to any condition in which victims suffered high temperatures and fever with no apparent cause. It was often described as 'infection of unknown origin', and it caused several of Robert's comrades to spent time in the field hospital, including the chaplain Cyril Francis.

given a tin of condensed milk. Each soldier was issued with waterproof matches and a pocket tin opener which could double as a spoon, and they used empty tins to boil their tea rations, swinging them around to settle the leaves.

Some letters might have told stories about how Robert and his comrades sang songs and wrote poems to keep their spirits up. They put on occasional concerts and Vera Lynn's *There'll Always Be an England* was a popular number, as was the George Formby song *Bless 'em All*, featuring the line 'you'll get no promotion this side of the ocean', to which the men invented their own, rather more lurid lyrics (although it's unlikely those were included in the letters). Several ditties from the first war were reintroduced by the veterans and songs like *Waltzing Matilda* and *Take Me Back to Dear Old Blighty* enjoyed a popular revival. As well as music, the men enjoyed games such as two-up and crown and anchor, which was forbidden, but they played anyway, betting for beer if they could get it.

There were many interesting characters among the troops, and Robert may have written about them and their exploits – such as when they renamed the main street of the nearby port town of Bardia from Rue de Mussolini to Rue de Ned Kelly. He might also have written about his commanding officer, Lieutenant Colonel Frederick Burrows. A veteran of the first World War, Lieutenant Colonel Burrows had served in Gallipoli and on the Western Front in France, and now led the 2/13th on its campaign in Egypt. He had a deep and robust voice which earned him the nickname 'The Bull', and it was he who led the battalion in its famous encounter at Er Regima. Unluckily, he received a gunshot wound to his head the next day, but he survived and returned to Australia where he was awarded the Distinguished Service Order, the Polish Cross of Valour, and a promotion to Brigadier.

Robert would have had plenty to say about the army chaplains, and there were certainly some eccentric characters among them – like the one who smuggled in a portable wind-up gramophone with his old record collection to play for the troops in the infirmary, or the one who said Mass in an air-raid shelter, ploughing ahead even though no one could hear the service over the enemy fire booming and crashing overhead.

The chaplains played a crucial role during the siege, not just as ministers of faith but in keeping up morale as well. Several denominations were represented – there were Catholic, Anglican, Methodist and Baptist ministers, and each took their turn braving enemy fire and landmines to conduct their ministry in far-off perimeter posts. They set up temporary churches in hospitals, tanks and dugouts, where they gave communion, heard confessions and performed any other spiritual ministrations that were necessary, including ministering to the Italian prisoners who didn't have their own priests with them. They received many appeals for compassionate leave from homesick men who wanted to return home to their wives and children, which they refused as sympathetically as they could. They were often to be found visiting camp hospitals, where they helped tend the wounded, comforted the sick and performed last rites for the dying. When necessary, they also helped with burial arrangements.

The priests and chaplains of the armed forces were very much active members of the crew and they shared living quarters with the soldiers, as did their assistants. They tended to work at a brigade rather than battalion level, so Robert's duties would have involved travelling with the padre from unit to unit, transporting a makeshift altar and any other equipment he required for communions, church parades or correspondence. They were often called upon by officers and generals who needed help with foreign documents, as the priests' knowledge of Latin made them useful translators. Robert would also have been responsible for maintaining his vehicle, which would have required protecting it as much as possible from the deterioration caused by heat, dust and wind. Being a batman was not without its dangers either – one Catholic Padre, a Patrick Reynolds, was on his way across the desert one day when an enemy shell shot through the back seat of his car and settled there without exploding. Fortunately no men were hurt and from that time on Father Reynolds had his drivers drop him off half-way so he could finish the journey on foot.

Despite the setbacks, the Allied defences continued to be effective and it was during this siege that the men involved came to the attention of one William Joyce, an American born Fascist politician more famously known in his time as 'Lord Haw-Haw'. He took German citizenship in 1940 and was well known as a Nazi propaganda broadcaster. He described the besieged men as 'living like rats in underground dugouts and caves' and referred to them as 'rats of Tobruk'. It was no doubt meant to be derogatory, but the Australians reclaimed the name and bore it with pride. They even struck their own official medal, bearing the likeness of a rat, with metal from one of the German bombers they had struck down.

By October, most of the original garrison was replaced by British, Czechoslovakian and Polish troops, although the 2/13th remained at the base and were therefore the only AIF battalion to see out the length of the siege. In November, they were involved in Operation Crusader – an attempt to recapture several positions held by the Axis armies. As part of the operation the Rats carried out several reconnaissance missions and one successful night raid on Ed Duda, in which they recaptured the city which had been lost earlier that day. The siege on Tobruk was finally lifted on December 10, and the port remained under allied control until it surrendered in June 1942.

There were, of course, regular reports from the frontlines to their superiors at home, and people on the home front looked to the newspapers and radio broadcasters for their daily updates. These included reports from

Tobruk – for example, this one which appeared in the Sydney Morning Herald on Monday, September 15, 1941:

> *"Our fighting patrols in the Tobruk area made deep penetrations into the enemy positions at a number of points without making contact. As the result of our activities, enemy shelling was particularly heavy in the eastern sector of Tobruk's defences. Enemy bombing attacks during the night were continuous, but there were no casualties and no important damage. Enemy patrols in the frontier area, moving somewhat wider than usual, are being successfully engaged. A Rome communiqué says: "There was considerable artillery activity on the land front in North Africa. Our air force bombed numerous sectors at Tobruk on the night of September 12-13, causing fires and explosions". Referring to activity in Abyssinia, a Rome communiqué says: "The enemy in the Gondar region bombed and machine-gunned a hospital hut marked with the Red Cross. Some persons were wounded. One of the attacking aircraft was shot down."*

Even if Kathleen had read this report, there was no way she could have known that Robert was stationed in Tobruk at the time, or whether or not he was involved in any of the engagements described. They relied on his letters for news of his wellbeing but not his whereabouts, and while they came in every month or so, they had no way to know if he was alive and well until the next one arrived.

Meanwhile in New South Wales, the government had raised the school leaving age to 14 and four months, so when she turned 14 in May, Marge was still in school. She was desperate to get out and into the workforce, but could do nothing about it until August, and even then her mother refused to allow her to leave school unless she had a job to go to. She would have loved to join the Women's Auxiliary Forces, an organisation set up in 1941 to help with the war effort and release men from certain roles so that they could be redeployed to the fighting units, but their minimum age was 18, so there was nothing she could do but wait. Fortunately, it so happened that Kathleen was queuing in the local butcher's shop one day when she overheard the butcher say to the lady in front of her, "I know of a job for your daughter", to which the lady replied "actually, my daughter has just found a job". Kathleen stepped in, and so it was that on August 4, 1941, Marge left high school and started a new job as an office assistant at Moran & Cato Pty Ltd.

This must have come as a surprise to the school headmistress, who had obviously noticed that Marge's attention had waned significantly over the past 18 months. She provided a reference stating that "she has not attained a high scholastic standard though she is a girl of fair ability who should have done better". She did, however, describe her as honest and reliable, and recommended that she "would do very well at some form of manual work, for she is sensible and practical."

The Bass Hill postmistress, a Mrs A Drewell, took a similar view of Marge's character, describing her as honest, trustworthy and reliable and coming from a "highly respectable family". However, she obviously had more faith in Marge's potential in the work force, declaring that "I feel with confidence she would give every satisfaction in whatever position she may hold."

Despite these differences of opinion one thing was clear: Marge was an honest, sensible and reliable 14-year-old, and the manager at Moran & Cato took her on without hesitation.

The next few months were a happy time in Marge's early life. She was finally free of school and homework (and the dreaded treadle machine) and was now an independent member of the workforce with a regular income. Each day she took a short bus ride to the station at Chester Hill, where she caught a train into Redfern in Sydney. From there it was a short walk to Cleveland Street in Chippendale to the offices of Moran & Cato.

Moran & Cato was a large grocery store chain founded by two cousins in Melbourne. By the 1940s they were the largest grocery chain in Australia with 120 branches in Victoria and Tasmania and 40 in New South Wales. Marge worked in an office with around 30 other girls, with their desks all lined up facing the same way and their manager sitting above them in a glass walled office so he could keep an eye on them. She could wear what she wanted now, and she dressed in lovely skirts, blouses and cardigans, all made by Kathleen, and some hand-me-downs from Bonny. She took her lunch with her every day, usually a sandwich and home-made cake or biscuits. It was a simple life, but it made her happy.

As an office assistant her job was to add up the figures that came in from the business's various stores and branches. She started each day with a pile of receipts and entered them into a machine, which was a bit like a calculator with a handle at the side which she pulled down to log each amount. From these she made totals and filed reports. Considering her best subjects at school had been arithmetic, business principles and bookkeeping, this job suited her perfectly and she loved it, and if there was anything that worried her she simply whispered Kathleen's words to herself, "there's no such word as can't." She also loved her new-found independence, but she was still only 14, as were many of the girls she worked with, so at the end of each day some of the men from the office escorted the girls back to the station where she repeated her journey via train and bus, and then back across the field to home where Kathleen always had her dinner ready.

Another perk of being in the workforce was that now she could go to the dances – as long as she could persuade Bonny to go with her. Bonny was a bookworm and more inclined to stay home with her head in a Mills & Boon novel, but persistent nagging from Marge usually won the day and each Saturday after dinner they did up each other's hair, put on their best frocks – made for them by Kathleen – and took the short bus ride to the Scout Hall. In 1941 the average weekly wage for an adult woman working full time was 57 shillings and 11 pence, or £2/17/11– (equivalent to about $240 today), which wasn't much, but as Kathleen was not working and they had only Robert's army wages to live on, every little bit helped. Each week Marge and Bonny kept two shillings for the dance plus whatever they needed for travelling to and from work, and gave the rest of their wages to Kathleen.

The dances were the highlight of Marge's week, and she looked forward to them with great excitement. Their two shillings paid for their entrance into the hall, refreshments – probably lemonade and sandwiches – and live music, usually from a local band made up of a piano, drums and a brass or wind instrument such as a clarinet, trumpet or saxophone. There was no alcohol served, since licensing laws in the 1940s prohibited the serving of alcohol after 6 p.m., and in any case most of the attendants were under the legal drinking age of 21. That didn't spoil the fun though, since they were familiar with all the dances, having learned them as children in the church hall while their mothers looked on with their sewing, and their absolute favourite song was Glenn Miller's *In The Mood*. Over time they got to know which boys were the better dancers and all the girls would wait around the edge of the hall in groups, hoping one of them would approach from the bunch standing at the back of the hall. It was all very proper and happened under close supervision, so Kathleen had no need to worry about them, although Marge often ended up dancing with more boys than she would have liked because she was always too kind to turn anyone down. At least it made her a better dancer and eventually she learnt the trick of securing the best partners, and how to disappear if she noticed one of the bad ones trying to catch her eye. They were heady days, and for Marge there was nothing better than the swell of the band, a nice boy to dance with and the swish of her frock as she swirled around the dance floor to a foxtrot or two-step.

Of course, as a pretty young girl there were always plenty of willing partners, but it just so happened that a particular group of young men caught her attention one evening. A group of sailors, still in their uniforms, were passing through town and must have learned about the dance, because they turned up in a flurry of navy and white charm and caused quite a stir among the young women. Marge and Bonny were so delighted to have such interesting and dashing companions for the evening that they completely lost track of time and missed the last bus home. Realising that they would have to walk several kilometres, the sailors offered to escort them and so of course it took much longer than it should have, because they talked and talked the whole way home. Instead of turning up at the usual time of 11.30 or midnight, it was nearly 2 o'clock by the time they were home, and if they thought the presence of a group of servicemen might reassure their mother, they were gravely mistaken. They tiptoed in but Kathleen was there waiting for them, sitting up in her chair by the fire. She had a few stern words to say and was not convinced by their explanation of how they got home, but fortunately they were still allowed to attend the dances. The sailors were never seen again, but Marge still looked forward to her night out every Saturday.

Alas, this idyllic time was not fated to last very long. By the beginning of 1942, Sydney Harbour had become a busy Allied naval base with several battle cruisers based there at any one time. Several local ferries had been converted into hospitals and troop carriers, and Garden Island, a narrow strip of land north east of the city, was being used as a temporary barracks for sailors transferring between ships. It was heavily defended with anti-submarine weapons and nets, and for many people the war was starting to feel a little close to home – especially with the recent Japanese attack on Pearl Harbour. People were becoming nervous, and many parents began sending their children inland to stay with relatives in the country. Kathleen considered sending her children away, but she couldn't bear to be parted from them and had no other reason to stay in Sydney, so in February 1942 she packed up her possessions, sold the family home and moved them all to Horsham in Victoria.

CHAPTER THREE

Worlds Away

* * *

Kathleen and her five children travelled on an overnight train from Sydney to Horsham, a journey of almost 700 kilometres. It must have been very tiring for Kathleen, and a bit sad for the children, who were leaving behind their friends, schools and jobs. But it was exciting too, and it helped that the train was full of soldiers travelling home on leave from Sydney – a source of great amusement to the four teenage girls, as well as to young Freddie who was nearly eleven by now. Apart from an occasional giggle or whisper they remained on their best behaviour, sitting politely on their cases because the train was full. Several passengers complimented Kathleen on her well-behaved children, and although they must have been tired by the time they arrived, the novelty of the journey and the mystery of the destination kept them up and alert to their new surroundings.

The train reached Horsham and they went to stay with some old friends of Kathleen's, Muriel and Fred Sanders. Muriel and Kathleen had been at school together, and the presence of her old friend was probably why Kathleen chose Horsham as the place to retreat with her children – it may even have been at Muriel's invitation. Mr and Mrs Sanders, or Aunty

Muriel and Uncle Fred as the children knew them, owned a farm about 20 kilometres outside Horsham between Quantong and Vectis East, and though they had no children of their own they were more than happy to accommodate the Stevensons until they had their own place. Victoria experienced a warm summer in 1942, and for a few happy weeks the children were free to explore and play outside without the pressure of time or commitments. They saw sheep for the first time, went for rides with Uncle Fred in the horse and dray (a small but heavy open wagon), climbed on the haystack and helped around the farm where they could. It was a carefree time, and they made the most of the warm days and mild evenings.

Another great novelty they experienced for the first time on the farm was a running shower, a real luxury after a routine of just one bath a week. They found it was very good for getting off any stray bits of hay that had got under their clothes, despite the limited supply from the nearby dam which meant they couldn't stay in for long as there might be up to seven people still waiting for a turn. There were also some more unpleasant things to adapt to, like the ever-present smell of animals, although that was nothing compared to the nasty smell of home-made butter which hadn't been washed enough! It was simply too much for Kathleen's usually well-mannered children, who couldn't help but hold their noses, much to their mother's embarrassment.

It seemed they were worlds away from the war and the tension in Sydney. They kept up to date by listening to the wireless in the evenings, and it was while they were on the farm that the news came on February 19 of the bombing of Darwin by the Japanese Navy, killing 230 people and destroying several buildings. It must have been a great to relief to Kathleen that she and the children were safely in the Victorian countryside, far away from Darwin or any other cities that may have posed a tempting target. They stayed for a few weeks with Muriel and Fred, until they found a house on Henry Street in Horsham and moved into the town.

It was time now for Kathleen and her family to start their new life and settle into a new neighbourhood. At that time Horsham was a small but prosperous centre of about 6,000 people, most of whom could date their ancestors' arrival and settlement to the gold rush years of the 1840s and 50s. Situated about 300 kilometres west of Melbourne on the floodplains of the Wimmera River, its position made it ideal for growing wheat, so by the time the Stevensons arrived it was a thriving agricultural hub surrounded by farmland on all sides.

Horsham in 1942 had all the features and amenities a young family could expect of a small town, including a railway, town hall, cinema, post office, shops and churches. Instead of markets there were general stores, and now Kathleen could walk into town and do all her shopping for groceries, homewares and fabric for clothes. Norma, Shirley and Freddie were enrolled in local schools, and as Kathleen still had her hands full at home, it was up to Bonny and Marge to find jobs and bring in a bit of extra income for the family.

Marge had a good reference from her manager at Moran & Cato, who described her as an 'honest and good worker' who 'leaves our employment of her own accord, and has carried out her duties to our satisfaction'. Armed with this glowing recommendation, she secured a position as a salesgirl at GJ Coles & Co Limited, a company known now for its grocery stores, but in 1942 ran a prosperous chain of general stores with branches in each state, sporting the slogan 'Nothing over 2/6'.* It was close enough for Marge to walk to work and back again, and even to walk home for lunch if she wanted to. Her timing was good – at the outbreak of war 95% of their male staff members had enlisted, so the opportunity was ripe for women to step up and take on roles that might not have otherwise

---

* Two shillings and six pence – about $10 in today's money.

been available. Bonny also gained a position at Coles, and they started on March 6.

Meanwhile, Robert was making his way back to Australia from the Middle East. At that time, several overseas battalions were being recalled to bolster the defence of the Northern Territory, but the first ship sent to retrieve them was sunk in the Mediterranean before it arrived, so the 2/13th was put on garrison duty in Syria while they waited for a replacement. During this time Robert was transferred to the 2/8th battalion, and when a ship finally did arrive to take them home, Robert went with them. They embarked on the TSS Aronda at Port Tewfik in Egypt on February 12 and set sail the next day, and unfortunately were still on route when the Japanese attacked Darwin a week later. Life on board followed a restricted but regular routine, with parades in the morning and training and drills adjusted to fit the small deck space. The men were woken by the reveille at 0600 hours, and hammocks had to be rolled and stacked by 0645 for breakfast at 0700. Troop decks were inspected before dinner at noon, and there were more drills before and after the evening meal at 1730. Lights went out at 2130, and every man was expected to be in his bed or hammock by 2145.

Most days the weather was hot and humid, with occasional heavy downpours which caused blackouts below decks, and at night there were allocated 'blackout' hours, when any lights, including the lighting of matches or cigarettes, was strictly forbidden anywhere on deck. Troops were ordered to wear soft soled shoes at all times so they wouldn't damage the deck, and under no circumstances were they to throw anything overboard, lest it be spotted by a hostile ship. There were regular alarm and life boat drills, there was Mass said on deck every Sunday and occasionally they were subjected to lectures on what standards were expected of them, such as when they were reprimanded for their over-use of foul language.

They had free time each day, and although gambling and diary keeping were forbidden, they could still play cards or write letters home, and fresh water was available at certain times each day for washing clothes. For entertainment the officers arranged regular boxing and wrestling tournaments which any man could enter, and on February 26 there was a concert and sing-song held on the promenade deck at 1800 hours. It was a suspended kind of life, away from all the action, and although they received regular news via telegrams there was nothing they could do except make sure they were ready for action when they landed. After stops in Colombo and Fremantle they landed in Adelaide on March 29, and from there they were billeted in Strathalbyn before travelling by train to the Northern Territory. By late May they were stationed at a base near the Adelaide River, about 120km south of Darwin, as part of the 19th Brigade.

The troops were positioned so that they could deploy on a broad front should there be another invasion on the north coast, though fortunately, despite several raids by the Japanese Navy Air Force on the islands, shipping routes and airspace, there never was another one as devastating as the first. In the meantime the troops remained on garrison duty, which may have involved anything from military parades and honour guards, assisting local authorities with community events, or helping manage disasters such as fires or floods. They would also have been expected to maintain a strict regime of exercise, training and drills, and several army units were involved in the building of military hospitals in Katherine and on the Adelaide River. Robert and his battalion remained in Darwin throughout 1942, waiting for an attack which fortunately (although perhaps frustratingly) never came.

Back in Horsham the war continued to feel much more distant than it had in Sydney. There were no more air raid drills, there were no garrisons stationed in the town and there was no presence of military craft or bases, so life took on a much more light-hearted mood. There was still a war effort – the local branch of the Red Cross, for example, held regular training sessions in First Aid, home nursing and other practical skills, and every so often, a train came through transporting soldiers to and from Sydney or Darwin, and the Red Cross set up a canteen at the station to serve them tea, coffee and food. They were usually joined by dozens or even hundreds of the local citizens, all hoping to get a look at the soldiers and creating something like a carnival atmosphere as they cheered and waved them on their way.

Meanwhile, Marge had settled in well to her new job – she worked on a cash register at the general store and enjoyed being out and about among people each day – and she and Bonny continued to give their mother most of their earnings, keeping, of course, the few shillings they needed each week for the dances. Being newcomers in a small town was not easy – it took time to make friends and it must have been particularly hard for Kathleen, who spent more time at home than the children did. She did have Muriel and Fred close by, and they saw each other often, and gradually she got to know people through the local church and groups such as the Country Women's Association. There were also the dance lessons at the church hall, and Kathleen sat with the other mothers, all doing their knitting as they chatted and watched the children. The dances themselves took place in the scout hall on Friday and Saturday nights, and for once being new did have some advantages. In a place where everyone knew everyone else and had been dancing with the same people for years, two new, pretty girls were something of a novelty and for a while they enjoyed a certain amount of attention from the boys in the town. It didn't take them long to figure out who the good partners were, and Kathleen kept them well supplied with frocks, blouses and cardigans so that they always looked their best.

As in Sydney, life in Horsham was simple but good, and when news came at the end of May that Japanese submarines had appeared in Sydney Harbour, Kathleen must have felt validated in her decision to move the family away. It wasn't a particularly successful attack – of the three subs that got into the harbour, one got tangled in anti-submarine nets and self-detonated, one was sunk and one was forced to retreat – but they did take down one ferry in the process, along with its 21 passengers, and Kathleen's sense of relief at being far away from any confrontation must have been great.

There was more change to come, however, with the introduction in June of the rationing of certain goods. Rationing in Australia was not as stringent or extreme as it was in the United Kingdom, since there was plenty of space for growing food, and the Japanese subs, although present, had a much more difficult time patrolling Australia's 60,000 kilometres of coastline than the German U-boats did patrolling Britain's 20,000. The measures were intended to curb inflation and limit shortages of essential goods such as clothing and foodstuffs, and in general it was successful. In 1942 the allowance per adult was set at ½ lb of tea every 5 weeks and 2lb of sugar per fortnight. Butter would be added to the ration list the following year, and meat the year after that. Milk and eggs were included from time to time, depending on supply, and each family was distributed a quota of coupons which they redeemed for their food items or saved up to buy clothes. The system worked, on the whole, although shortages remained after the war and the rationing system was gradually phased out between 1947 and 1950.

1943 arrived, and with it more changes. Marge had received a promotion at work and was now working as a secretary, after the previous holder of the position had married a Colonel and followed him to a new post in Sydney. She'd applied for the vacant position and got it, despite never having used a typewriter before, and she taught herself to compose letters by copying older ones that were already on file. Usually these were notices to customers informing them about their orders and deliveries, and sometimes she took dictation from the manager and helped him with his correspondence. She was also responsible for the money in the store: every evening she had to tally up the profits from the tills, make up the floats for the next morning, which she locked in the safe, and give the rest to the manager who took it to the bank. In the mornings she handed out the floats to the girls on the tills, and once a week she made up the pay for all the staff. It was work she was well suited to and had an aptitude for, and it gave her a great sense of fulfilment.

She got on well with her manager, Mr Robinson, despite his being fond of a drink and rather laid-back when it came to his own attendance at the office. He was often missing when important things happened or decisions had to be made, and it was Marge who had to track him down – usually by calling his wife – and he was more often than not found unwinding in the pub with a certain Mr Bonwick, the man who owned the jewellers next door. He was a good boss though, and trusted Marge, even giving her the nickname 'Junior'. She made friends with the girls she worked with, and as well as seeing them at the dances each week she even joined them to play basketball some mornings. She wasn't very good – mainly because she couldn't see the ball most of the time – but she enjoyed the activity and the company of young women her own age.

Unfortunately by this time her sister Bonny was no longer working at Coles – she hadn't got on very well with Mr Robinson's predecessor and they had had frequent altercations, culminating in an argument one day when he swore at her about something, and she had the unfortunate bad sense to swear back. She lost her job, but found work at Langlands, another department store on the corner of Firebrace and Wilson Streets, which had the distinction of being the town's first post office. She worked in their shoe department for a while before taking a job at a canvas factory making parachutes and tents for the war.

Letters from Robert would have contained more news now too – in May 1943, after a year in the Northern Territory, he was once again transferred, this time to the 2/4th Battalion, which was then transferred to Queensland. The 2/4th was part of the same brigade that had been stationed in Darwin and had also been brought home from the Middle East. Both battalions were transferred to Queensland after the return to the Northern Territory of troops from New Guinea, which had just been relieved by American troops. On May 30 they were woken at 0230 to embark on the HMT Duntroon, and they set sail from the port of Larrakeyah in Darwin on the 31st.

They disembarked in Brisbane on June 8 and were granted two weeks leave, in which Robert returned to Victoria before being stationed at Wondecla in Queensland, about a hundred kilometres southwest of Cairns near the Atherton Tablelands. Here Robert underwent more training, until at the end of September he was transferred to the 16th Australian Army Personnel Staging Camp, more commonly known as the Redlynch Staging Camp, near Cairns. Redlynch was a busy military hub through which thousands of soldiers passed during the war years, collecting mail, rations and supplies and enjoying a short rest before being sent on to the front lines. However, Robert was sent from Redlynch to the LHQ Training Centre in Canungra, an hour or so south of Brisbane in the Macpherson Ranges.

The centre – now known as the Land Warfare Centre – was set up in 1942 as a jungle training camp in response to the need for troops in the southwest Pacific. Units here spent four weeks learning bushcraft and survival techniques, and special units who would become Independent

Company reinforcements stayed an additional four weeks. Independent companies were special commando-style units that were tasked with specific and special operations such as raids, demolitions, sabotage, subversion and organising civil resistance. Most of the Australian independent companies who trained at Canungra were subsequently deployed in New Guinea.

It is unclear from Robert's records how much time he spent in Canungra, but it's likely that he remained there for the duration of the war, probably working as a driver for the HQ 1 Recruit Training Battalion that was based there. He must have got himself into a few scrapes, as at the end of June 1944 he was evacuated to the 22nd Australian Camp Hospital in Tamborine, just 20 kilometres from Canungra, with a 'foreign body' in his right arm. He was there for three weeks before rejoining his unit on August 19. A month later he was given a medical assessment and classified in the level B2 – this meant that he could see and hear sufficiently well for ordinary purposes, was permitted a walk of up to five miles to and from work, but could not serve on the front lines. As he was now 38 years old and had been having trouble with his back, this was probably not much of a surprise, and his duties from this time onwards were most likely limited to driving and transporting goods and troops between bases and training centres.

Being in Canungra would have given Robert some interesting stories to put in his letters. The training there was intense – it was designed to mimic jungle combat conditions and only those physically fit enough could complete it. For the first three weeks, they trained for 12 hours a day, six days a week, and this included shooting exercises, obstacle courses and moving through all terrains (including crossing rivers) in full kit. Then in their fourth week of training they were sent on a six-day training exercise into the Macpherson Ranges, with each man carrying his own provisions. Robert may not have completed the training himself, but

Chapter Three – Worlds Away

there would have been lots to write about: the intense humidity, looking out for leeches, climbing through the mud and having to clean it out of clothes and equipment. He might have written about sleeping outside in the rainforest, the sounds of birds and insects at night, and the stars he glimpsed through the jungle canopy. Perhaps he would have mentioned his new comrades, now that he was in a new battalion, or told stories of the commanding officer of the camp, a Lieutenant-Colonel 'Bandy' MacDonald. It's likely, too, that he ran into some of his old comrades of the 2/13th, as many of them came through the Queensland training camps on their way to deployment in New Guinea and Borneo.

The mud of Canungra was a world away from the sand and dust of Libya, but soldiers were the same everywhere, and they always had ways to entertain themselves when they were off duty. It's easy to imagine a platoon of 2,000 or more exhausted soldiers lounging around the camp canteen, sharing tobacco rations, playing cards, writing letters or cleaning their boots and equipment. Each day they would line up for meals and the only sound for a while would be the clink of spoons and forks against the metal dishes as each man tucked into plain but welcome fare. They could look forward to canteen day and movie night once a week, and Robert could easily have written about how they would crowd together in a darkened room, watching Charlie Chaplin in *The Great Dictator*, Humphrey Bogart in *Casablanca* or Judy Garland in *Meet Me in St Louis* – each one would have been a welcome distraction from the world and the war outside.

A letter arriving in Horsham was always a welcome event for the family, who knew that Robert was somewhere in Australia, and that was all. They read the letters together, sitting around the wireless in the evenings, listening to the news and speculating about what the gaps in the letters concealed. Sometimes Fred and Muriel joined them, and another old friend of Kathleen's who they called Granny Wise. Granny Wise taught the children to play poker with pennies, which Kathleen tolerated despite claiming it would end it tears. She was right of course, because someone always lost their pennies, but they were always happy to have another game – it just had to be packed away very quickly if the minister or someone else came to call. The younger children had their homework, and Marge helped her mother make socks for the soldiers by doing most of the knitting and then passing them to Kathleen to turn the heel and toe. They put parcels together for Robert, too, mostly cakes, biscuits and letters, and these were wrapped in calico, placed in a tin and sent off with the socks to wherever he was at the time.

They enjoyed the music too, and often sat together with Fred and Muriel, singing along to songs like *Good Luck, Cheerio, We'll Meet Again* or *The Boogie Woogie Bugle Boy*. Somehow, knowing they were singing the same songs as the people in England gave them a sense of solidarity with their mother country that was suffering so much more than they were, and with the men on the front lines who were so far from home. It helped to think they might be cheering them on a bit and contributing to the war effort in their own small way.

Churchill's voice was also a familiar one, as all his speeches were relayed over the Australian airwaves, and it gave them hope to know that their allies in Europe were not giving up. It was some years now since his famous words "We shall never surrender", and as the war spread across the globe to America and the Pacific, it was reassuring to hear that they were not forgotten, that he pledged to come to their aid as soon as the Nazis were defeated:

> *"It is our duty to peer through the mists of the future to the end of the war, and to try our utmost to be prepared… I can imagine*

that some time next year — but it may well be the year after — we might beat Hitler, by which I mean beat him and his powers of evil into death, dust, and ashes. Then we shall immediately proceed to transport all the necessary additional forces and apparatus to the other side of the world to punish the greedy, cruel Empire of Japan, to rescue China from her long torment, to free our territory and that of our Dutch allies, and to drive the Japanese menace forever from Australian, New Zealand, and Indian shores."

The wireless was their main form of entertainment in the evenings as well, and in the 1940s there were several young stars bursting onto the scene with all the optimism of the youth of the day. Music tastes were shifting from jazz and ragtime to big band swing, and *In The Mood* remained Marge's firm favourite. Glen Miller and Joe Loss, with their famous orchestras, dominated those early years of the decade, and Judy Garland, Vera Lynn and the Andrews Sisters kept spirits up with their stirring, patriotic numbers. Then in July, 1942 Bing Crosby's *White Christmas* erupted on to the airwaves, starting a new trend that would brighten up Christmas radio for the next several years; Frank Sinatra, Dean Martin and Ella Fitzgerald were quick to follow suit. In their busy lives, listening to the wireless was the one thing that brought the family together, and despite the ever-present threat of the war and worry about Robert, life passed as happily as it could in troubled times.

There were things in their own lives to look forward to as well, and on April 9, 1945, the family celebrated the wedding of Marge's sister Bonny to Eric Dooling, the owner of a local bike shop. Robert was granted leave for the occasion and arrived from Queensland in time to give his eldest daughter away, walking her proudly down the aisle of St John's church in Horsham, although perhaps with a slight limp, caused by an injury to his right thigh. Bonny made a beautiful bride, in a long white dress with an A-line skirt, with a pinched waist and enormous, puffed sleeves which were the height of fashion at the time. Marge and Shirley, as the proud bridesmaids, wore dresses of soft blue, with pleats gathered from the shoulder to create a V-line neck. They had long, gathered skirts that flowed when they moved, and small bouquets of blue flowers. Norma finished off the party in a light pink satin dress, and all of them wore white gloves and were made up with lipstick and rouge. After the ceremony there was a party in the church hall, complete with afternoon tea and plenty of dancing. There were children from Eric's side, and they sat at their own table with their plates of pretty cakes and fairy bread.

A few weeks after that, on May 1, Marge turned 18 and was now old enough to join the Women's Auxiliary Services if she wished, but she was enjoying her work and didn't like to leave her mother, especially now that Bonny was married and her father had returned to his unit. He'd only been granted a short leave, and was back in Queensland less than a week after the wedding – before Bonny and Eric returned from their honeymoon. So Marge decided to stay where she was, at least for now.

On the same day, Robert arrived back at Canungra after having spent another two weeks at the camp hospital. A week after his discharge, on the 8th, the Germans finally surrendered to the Allies, and three months later on August 15 – a week after the bombing of Hiroshima – Japan followed suit, finally ending the conflict in the Pacific. On the same day, Robert was granted a proficiency pay, and on October 9 he was cleared to return to Sydney. He was formally discharged from service on October 23, after serving a total of 1,980 days in the Middle East and Australia. Kathleen and the children could finally look forward to his coming home for good.

CHAPTER FOUR

Our Men and Women Will Come Home

***

At 9:30 a.m. on Wednesday, 15 August, 1945, the citizens of Australia stood still, huddled around radios and wirelesses around the nation as the British Prime Minister, Clement Attlee, delivered the joyous news they had all been waiting for:

> "Japan has today surrendered. The last of our enemy is laid low. Peace has once again come to the world. Let us thank God for this great deliverance and his mercies. Long Live the King."

Scenes of jubilation followed this speech. Desks and registers were abandoned as civilians and service personnel alike rushed into the streets, cheering and singing and waving flags. Traffic came to a standstill in the cities as the streets filled with revellers, blowing whistles and swinging rattles in a noisy surge of euphoria. Car horns tooted and blared all over the country and streamers were hung from every building. In Sydney, some exuberant Scots danced a highland fling around the Cenotaph while a group of girls danced the hokey pokey with a troop of sailors, and in Martin Place a giant dummy of Adolf Hitler was lowered into the street and 'hung' from a building. Worries were forgotten, cares abandoned and concerns banished. Enemies became friends and strangers became comrades. It was a time, for one day at least, only for celebration, and in the words of one ABC reporter, Talbot Duckmanton, they had 'a whale of a time'.

There were quiet moments too, and Mr Duckmanton described, for those listening in, the fresh wreaths which had been laid at the Cenotaph and the people who gathered round, removing their hats reverently. "Sydney, despite all this gaiety and rejoicing at the news of the Japanese surrender, has not forgotten that our men, and our allies too, have paid a high price, so that we may rejoice in this way," he said.

At some point during the day, those who had remained near their radios would have heard an address from the new Australian Prime Minister, Benedict Chifley, in which he expressed his regret that his predecessor – the late John Curtin, who had led Australia through most of the war until his death in July of that year – and the late American leader Mr Roosevelt had not lived to see this day. He thanked the fighting forces, as well as those who had supported the war effort on the home front, and urged his country to carry on the work to make the peace a lasting one:

> *"Hello citizens. The War is over. The Japanese government has accepted the terms of surrender imposed by the allied nations, and hostilities will now cease... At this moment let us offer thanks to God, let us remember those whose lives were given that we may enjoy this glorious moment, and may we look forward to a peace which they have won for us. Let us remember those whose thoughts, with proud sorrow, turn towards gallant loved ones who will not come back. On behalf of the people and the government of Australia, I offer humble thanks to the fighting men of the United Nations, whose gallantry, sacrifice and devotion to duty have brought us the victory. Nothing can fully repay the debt we owe them, nor can history record in adequate*

terms their deeds that followed the black days in September 1939 and December 1941 until this moment.

"And now our men and women will come home; our fighting men, with battle honours thick upon them from every theatre of war. Australians stopped the Japanese and their drive south, just as they helped start the first march toward ultimate victory in North Africa. Australians fought in the battles of the air everywhere, and Australian seamen covered every ocean. They are coming home to a peace which has to be won. The United Nations charter for a world organisation is the hope of the world, and Australia has pledged the same activity in making it successful as she's shown in the framing of it.

"You are aware of what has been arranged for the celebration of this great victory and deliverance. In the name of the Commonwealth Government, I invite you to join in the thanksgiving services arranged, for truly this is a time to give thanks to God, and for those men against whose sacrifice for us there is no comparison. Good day to you, fellow citizens."

The United Nations he mentioned was then a fledgling organisation with a charter that had been adopted only a couple of months before and drafted by the 'big four' allied nations, as they were known: the United Kingdom, the United States, the Soviet Union and China. When it took effect in October that year there were 51 initial member states, and Australia was one of them. The UN was the hope of the new world with its objectives of maintaining peace, protecting human rights, delivering humanitarian aid and upholding international law. Such a collective effort by the world's nations had never been achieved before, and finally people could dream of a peaceful future.

Meanwhile in Horsham, celebrations were no less subdued. Marge and her colleagues, after listening to the news on the office radio, dropped what they were doing and headed out into the streets like everyone else, dancing and singing and celebrating with the rest of the nation. The fire brigade rang its sirens throughout the day and into the night, bells pealed from the churches and schools and boys tied metal tins to their bicycles which they clattered through the streets. The Horsham Town Band filled the air with patriotic medleys and strangers linked arms to dance the Lambeth Walk to the sounds of the Horsham Pipe Band. Shop windows were decorated in red, white and blue, with some flying allied flags or sporting pictures of the royal family. Someone even dressed up a big white bulldog with a Union Jack in its collar.

At 12 o'clock, the Mayor, Councillor L. Hutchesson, addressed the people from the balcony of the Town Hall in Wilson Street, saying that he was sure they were all rejoicing at the news of the cessation of hostilities and reminding them of those that 'still need our sympathy and prayers'. He then called for three victory cheers, which rang out around the town.

Meanwhile, in the nearby law courts, the day's session ploughed on despite the noise and disturbance from outside – much to the chagrin, it must be imagined, of the poor souls inside. The judge kept them until 4 p.m. when the children's court was due to open, when he finally declared 'I think we have had enough today. No doubt those present want to see some of the fun going on outside.' The courtroom was deserted in seconds.

In the evening many people held private parties and the Horsham Pipe Band and Apex Club held a dance at the Masonic Hall. In Firebrace Street shop windows, verandas and neon lights were lit for the throngs of people who were still celebrating outside. The following day citizens crammed into the Town Hall for a thanksgiving service, and the Horsham Town band paid a visit to the Horsham Base Hospital to play for the patients and staff. Amazingly, no acts of vandalism or any 'untoward incidents' were reported to police, and the local paper was pleased to announce it had been a 'well behaved crowd' that had gathered in the streets on the 15th. Not much work had got done that day, but that didn't matter at all – for one day at least, normal life was suspended.

Eventually, of course, celebrations subsided and day to day life resumed, but the aftermath of the war would be long. In the Pacific the fighting forces were being disbanded and gradually the men began to return home. Not all of them did, of course – of the nearly one million Australian men and women who served in the war, over 27,000 were either killed in action or died as a result of disease or accidents. Many families had lost two or even more family members to the war, and the joy felt as husbands and fathers returned home was tempered by the knowledge that others had not been so lucky. In every city and town around the country, names and dates were added to the war memorials, and new ones were built.

In Horsham a 'Welcome Home Committee' was formed and its first task was to arrange a series of Welcome Home functions at the Town Hall, which would be jointly hosted by the Mayor, the RSL, the Fathers' Association and the local churches, represented by the Rev. Father O'Bryan. At the first event, held on October 19, Mr R.J. Wilmoth, the president of the local branch of the Fathers' Association, officially welcomed the first ex-servicemen and women back to Horsham:

> *"Six years ago I had the honour, on behalf of the citizens, of farewelling the boys who left Horsham, not knowing where they were going. During that time, whatever the odds, they fought in the snows of Greece, in the sands of Tobruk, the valleys of Crete, the mountains of Syria. Later they came back to fight in New Guinea and in Borneo where they showed the same magnificent*

courage. Now, six years later, we have the much happier task of welcoming those who are coming back to their homes."

The President of the Horsham RSL, Mr O.M. Yule, also welcomed them back and promised that the RSL would provide assistance to returned soldiers in finding employment and readjusting to civilian life. The Mayor then promised that 60% of new State Housing Commission homes would be allocated to returned soldiers. A couple of weeks later, on October 31, a service was held in the town hall for the dedication of a miniature shrine of remembrance, which would be presented to the Fathers' Association. It was led by the padre J Fairlie Forrest, who had himself served and spent several years as a German prisoner of war, and on it was inscribed the names of 38 local men who would not be returning home.

Meanwhile Kathleen, Marge and the family had been in Horsham for almost four years – long enough to know several families who had lost loved ones. They were fortunate though, and in due course Kathleen received a telegram from the army offices in Sydney notifying her that Robert had been discharged. They waited with anticipation and excitement, and it must have been a great relief to Kathleen to think she could once again share the burden of raising and supporting her five children.

But as the men returned, and other families were reunited with their husbands, fathers, sons and brothers, it became apparent that something was amiss. The trains arrived, transporting men from Sydney to Darwin, Adelaide and beyond as they had always done, but Robert was not on them. Men stepped off to greet their families waiting on the platform, but the Stevensons were left waiting.

Weeks turned into months and still there was no sign of him. Kathleen wrote, but received no reply. She contacted the Army offices, but if they knew his location they did not disclose it. Old friends that she contacted either hadn't heard, or wouldn't say. Even his family didn't know where he was. Robert, it seemed, had disappeared.

1945 turned into 1946, and still he did not appear. Kathleen and the children carried on with their lives, going to work and school, and church, where the other families sat happily, their sons and fathers returned to them. It was a strange kind of time, and they found themselves on the outside of a society that preferred order and predictability. They could not share in the grief of the families who had lost loved ones, nor the joy of those reunited. They could only wait, while around them the whispers grew louder and the stares more pronounced.

Kathleen carried on stoically, and if she had any knowledge or theories about what had happened to her husband she did not share them with her children. Eventually she had no choice but to accept the inevitable truth – Robert was not coming back. It was a devastating blow, but any feelings of anger, sadness, grief or betrayal had to be pushed aside, because she had a much more urgent problem to deal with – the sudden lack of income. Since Robert had been discharged the army wages had stopped coming in, but as he was still alive Kathleen was not entitled to a pension. She would have to find a way to support the family on her own, and so she did.

She secured a job in a local bakery where she could work during the day and where her cooking skills would once again prove to be very useful. Each day after seeing off the children with their lunches she walked in to the cafe, worked the lunch shift and then walked home, where she always had dinner ready for everyone when they got home from work or school. After a few months – probably once the children had all left school and got jobs – she took a second job at Perrin's cafe cooking for weddings and functions in the evenings.

She took in some boarders too, since the large house had plenty of spare rooms. These were mainly young men from the country who moved into town to work and gave Kathleen money for their room and board. Once again her skills at making food stretch a long way came in useful, and the continuation of the rationing system meant that at least they didn't go without certain essentials. Fred and Muriel were a great support to her during this time, coming into town to visit the family each week and bringing vegetables from the farm, or fruit which Kathleen turned into jams and preserves.

It's possible that at this time she may also have applied for help from the government. A Widows' Pension had been introduced in 1942, and it also applied to abandoned wives – as long as they could prove that they'd taken reasonable measures to obtain maintenance from their husband. Even if she had received the pension, by September 1945 it was a tiny £1/17/6 a week – less than a quarter of the average working man's wage. Whether she applied for or obtained the pension or not is unknown, but there can be no doubt that Kathleen was a very resourceful woman.

Bonny was now married and therefore no longer working, but Marge continued to give her mother most of her wages, and as her sisters left school and found work, they did the same. Shirley got a job at Audene's, an exclusive dress shop and manufacturer that specialised in lingerie and hosiery, and every day she went off to work in her best clothes and make-up, along with requests from her sisters for any products they wished to purchase at a discount. Norma was the last of the girls to leave school and she took a job as a telephonist at the post office, connecting inbound calls with their onward destinations via an enormous switchboard. Freddie left school eventually and took a job at Paterson's Furniture store as a carpet and flooring layer, but the absence of his father for almost half his life was beginning to take its toll. Now a teenager and with income of his own, he spent more and more time away from his family. It must have been a great worry to Kathleen, who had probably been hoping that the return of his father might settle him down a little bit. At least she could still provide him with a stable home, and he did usually make it home for Sunday lunch.

By now Marge had also taken a second job as an usherette at the small theatre in Horsham, and the extra money was more valued than ever. Fortunately she loved the job, as she got to wear a long frock and was usually allocated the balcony area, where people were slightly better behaved. Feature films were often preceded by a curtain raiser of news and current affairs reels, and while the war was on theatres played clips of the fighting or small films from stations and bases overseas. As a subject the war filled people's imaginations and as a result it set the background for many big films of the early '40s. After the war the trend began to change, and more light-hearted, escapist films such as *Beauty and the Beast*, *It's a Wonderful Life* and Disney's *Song of the South* did spectacularly well at the box office. Hitchcock began making waves in Hollywood with films like *Notorious* and *The Paradise Case*, and the big names of the day included Rita Hayworth, Bette Grable, Lana Turner, Olivia de Havilland and Ingrid Bergman. Marge's job was to show theatregoers to their seats, after which she was allowed to stay and watch the films – a wonderful opportunity, since she could not afford to see them otherwise. But more often than not, after showing the guests back to their seats after the interval, she tiptoed out of the cinema and went to join her friends at the dances.

On the evenings when she wasn't working or at the dances Marge joined her family and the boarders at home, where they sat together after dinner listening to the wireless and working on hobbies or crafts. By now Marge had also taken on some knitting jobs and she worked away with the needles in her lunch breaks and in the evenings for a bit of extra money. The news on the wireless would have been strikingly different now – instead of updates on battles, reports of campaigns or statistics about casualties abroad, there was news of continuing war trials in Europe, the British Empire's struggles in India and the Soviet Union tightening its grip on Eastern Europe – not to mention the tricky decisions that had to be made regarding what to do about the atomic bomb, which had proven to be a little too spectacularly effective.

There was good news, too: in 1946 the world turned its eyes toward the future and looked further into space than it ever had before with the invention of the Hubble telescope. In January, the United Nations held its first General Assembly and in March France finally granted independence to Vietnam. Nat King Cole and his jazz trio dominated the airwaves, paving the way for several African American artists to follow, and 1946 also saw the invention of that enduring staple of every homemaker's kitchen – Tupperware.

In summer there was cricket on the radio too, and Marge and her sisters were greatly entertained by the commentators who used different props to make sounds for hits, catches and run outs. In the summer of 1946-47, to great anticipation, Donald Bradman returned to the game after an absence of eight years against Australia's old rivals the English. After a slow start, he scored 187 in his first innings and dominated the series, which Australia won 3-0. He returned the following summer for one last season, finishing with his final infamous dismissal for a duck and a test average of 99.94. It must have been a welcome change to sit around the wireless together in peace time, joining in songs about love rather than war, hearing news of the world coming together for the first time, and the thrilling antics of 'The Don' as they guessed at all the clicks and clunks coming from the commentary. Times were indeed changing for the better.

Of course, all of this did not take away the fact that their husband and father, who should have been enjoying those times with them, was not there. Kathleen took the loss of her childhood sweetheart very hard, and although she made a great success of supporting her family on her own, it wasn't easy and she couldn't give in to despair or sadness because the children were depending on her to hold things together. The girls missed him too, but they had plenty going on to distract them and as he had not been the most affectionate or loving of fathers, and he had been absent from their lives for the better part of five years anyway, perhaps the loss was easier to bear. For Marge at least – who understood, as her mother had, that there was nothing to do but get on with things – initial feelings of shock and betrayal gave way to anger and sorrow, until eventually these passed and she came to peace with it. Bonny had been closer to him and missed him more keenly, and for Freddie, who was now the only male in the family, it was a sharp blow.

Eventually, each in their own time came to accept he was not coming back, and as a family unit they remained close. This was a good thing, because in a small town in 1946 it was not so easy to avoid the watchful eyes of the local gossips, and for Kathleen it was impossible to escape the stigma that attached itself to abandoned and divorced women. She couldn't help noticing that invitations that once had poured in had begun to dry up, nor could she deny the loneliness she felt when she saw other couples out walking together. But she was a strong woman, as were her daughters, and they refused to shut themselves away. They continued to work, go to church and attend community events and fundraisers, and if they resented their circumstances they didn't let it show. Time passed, and the family became closer than ever.

Despite the hardships, life was full of opportunity. Marge was enjoying her work, her country was at peace and there was still plenty of fun to be had. Bonny and Eric were living close by on Rose Street, an easy half hour-walk away which took them through Horsham's Central Park, so they saw each other often, and in July that year Marge became an aunty to Yvonne,

Bonny's first daughter. On summer weekends the girls and Freddie often cycled out to Green Lake, about half an hour from Horsham, with a picnic lunch packed for them by Kathleen. Cycling in dresses was a nuisance, but the bikes had special guards on the back wheels which stopped skirts from getting caught and fortunately fashions were changing – Kathleen acquired patterns for shorts and sewed them each a pair, so they could zoom along without worrying about their clothes getting stuck in a wheel spoke. The 1940s also saw the advent of the bikini, and Kathleen knitted these for the girls as well. On a warm summer's day there was nothing better than sitting by the lake with their sandwiches and cakes, perhaps throwing a ball or frisbee, and then jumping in the lake to cool off. Bonny and Eric often joined them, riding up on Eric's motorbike with Bonny in the sidecar holding the baby, and sometimes Marge went with her friends from work, to play tennis on the shore before going for a swim and then drying off as they rode home. Unfortunately the swim suits were woollen, which made them scratchy out of the water and heavy and cumbersome in it, but that was a small price to pay and they savoured the freedom and independence of those carefree days.

For Marge, who was never one to dwell on hardships, there was always something to look forward to, and the thing she looked forward to the most was the dances. These were occasions where young people could gather and forget about the troubles of the world around them, and now Shirley and Norma were old enough to join her. The music scene was still changing, and the American influence in the war years saw the rise in popularity of jazz and swing numbers with their upbeat melodies and energetic steps and turns, which Marge loved. When the music paused they would take refreshments, and the boys would disappear for a short time to drink a few smuggled beers from the backs of their cars.

The dances were also a chance to get dressed up, and Kathleen continued to make clothes and dresses for them. Women's fashions were now changing too, and as more and more women joined the workforce they shifted towards the hourglass shape, and girls wore dresses with padded shoulders and nipped in waists. Skirts came to just below the knee, and as swing dancing caught on – with its fast footwork and quick turns – they began to flare outwards, and several layers underneath created a colourful effect when they spun on the dance floor. Echoing the business style that women were becoming accustomed to, dresses began to appear with short sleeves, short collars and buttons down the front – although they were still worn with hats and gloves. Most women wore court shoes with a small heel, although the younger girls like Marge still preferred flat shoes that were easier to dance in.

It was only a matter of time before the boys began to see Marge as something more than a potential dance partner, and in those first few years in Horsham she had many suitors. In those days, there was a strict code of etiquette that dictated how any courtship should proceed. A young man who invited a lady to a dance was expected to meet her at her home and then either walk or drive her to the dance. He should also see her home at the end of the evening, taking care not to be too late in case there was an angry parent waiting on the doorstep when they got there. If the young man was lucky he might get a kiss on the cheek before she went in, or perhaps the promise of another date. For the girl's part, if she went to a dance with a young man she was expected to save him the first and last dances, and ideally several in between. If she was on a date it was still acceptable to dance with others during the evening, but she should have the most dances with her date, and perhaps allow him to lend her his jacket. If she was there unaccompanied she could dance with whoever she wished, and though it was not polite to say no if you were asked, there were ways of avoiding those you didn't like very much or weren't good dancers. It was generally accepted that whoever you had the last dance with should walk you home, so these were hotly contested by the available young men.

Marge had many offers in those early days. There was one young man who she entered several dance competitions with, and another who took her horse riding, despite her being terrified of horses. Another boy she wasn't so keen on asked her out several times before she finally said yes, because his mother was a friend of Kathleen's and she was very insistent. Unfortunately for him it didn't progress further than one trip to the movies, when she was naturally unimpressed with the one Lion mint he offered her at the interval.

Then there was a young man called Jack McCarthy, who she became good friends with. He was an exceptional dancer, and they always danced the first and last dances together – a clear indicator to others in the room that the two of them were courting. They spent time together on the weekends, went to the movies, and got to know each other's families quite well. To anyone looking from the outside, it seemed as if things were serious indeed.

But Marge at this point was still only 17 – she was not ready to be tied down and despite having a settled and ordered life that she was happy with, she had an adventurous streak that the kind and steady Jack McCarthy couldn't quite live up to. Eventually the relationship came to a natural end, much to Jack's disappointment. Marge was once again free to accept invitations from whoever she wished, and she was still young enough to be able to take her time about it.

It was an unwritten rule in the 1940s that girls should be married by the age of 21, and if you didn't meet someone at the dances then your options were limited. Fortunately, Horsham was the biggest town for many miles around, and young people from the surrounding towns and villages often made the trip for these social events, which widened the pool of potential partners significantly. These smaller towns also held their own dances, but as Marge had no way to get to them she and her friends kept mostly to the dances in Horsham and were happy to meet men from the other towns that way. Of course, sometimes they were invited further afield, and if they had a way to get there and back again they were usually willing to go. Little did Marge realise there would soon be an invitation which would lead to an adventure better than she could ever have expected.

CHAPTER FIVE

Corporal Stevens

* * *

William John Stevens, known to everyone as Jack, was born on May 9, 1922 in Moyston, near Ararat in Victoria. He was the fifth of nine children, and the second son of Frederick Thomas Stevens and Katherine Jean MacLeod. Frederick and Katherine, although both from large families themselves, had very different backgrounds. Frederick, the third child of William Stevens and Mary Talbot, was born in 1888 at Pyramid Hill, about 85 kilometres north of Bendigo in Victoria. His youngest sister, Julia, was born two years later, and that same year his father died at the age of only 35, leaving Mary a widow with four children, of whom the eldest, Ethel, was only five. It must have been a difficult childhood for Frederick, without a father figure to learn from and depending on friends and other family members for help and support.

Katherine, on the other hand, was the fourth of eight children. Her parents were James McLeod of Bonor Bridge in Scotland, and Jessie Brookhouse of Fulham in London. They were married in 1888 and migrated to Australia soon afterwards, where they moved around for a few years before settling in Cranbourne in Victoria. They had six girls before being blessed with a boy, James, in 1905, and fifteen years later another boy,

David, came along. There were 22 years between the eldest and youngest, and all survived to adulthood except the fifth daughter, Evelyn, who died in 1900 aged two. Katherine, who was known to everyone as Kitty, was born in Avenel in 1895 before her parents settled in Cranbourne, and it must have been a happy childhood, being surrounded by sisters and having two baby brothers to dote on. Both her parents lived into their 70s – James died in 1933 aged 77, and Jessie died in 1941 aged 71.

Fred and Kitty married in Collingwood in 1914 when Fred was 26 and Kitty was 18. They spent time in Cranbourne, Berwick, Ararat and Moyston before settling in Murtoa with their six children, in a house on Friend Street at the southern end of town by Lake Marma. They soon settled in and became well known around the town – Frederick found work as a shearing contractor at nearby Sudholz Farm and Kitty joined many groups and societies, her quiet and homely disposition earning her many friends. They had three more children in Murtoa – the youngest, June, was 19 years younger than her eldest sister, Jean.

Jack was a clever and mischievous boy, and particularly devoted to his elder brother, named Frederick for his father but known to everyone as Jim. There were only two years between them, and the two of them were often coming up with schemes to earn pocket money or make their lives easier, but most of the time they only ended up getting into trouble – such as the time when they stole a duck from the local pub, thinking that it would provide their mother with some extra eggs. They took it home on the bike, one riding while the other held the duck, and were very disappointed when their mother sent them straight back to return it and apologise.

Jack was also excellent with numbers, and despite coming from a family of labourers he was assured, early in his life, that he would never have to work with his hands. His teachers probably expected him to pursue a career in finance or perhaps teaching, but the imminent prospect of war and limited finances meant opportunities were scarce, and so despite showing such promise Jack left school early in his teens and joined his father and brother in the shearing trade, taking a job at Sudholz farm and giving all his wages back to his parents. When the war broke out in 1939 he was only 17 – much too young to enlist, although the lure of travel and adventure overseas must have been tempting to a young man who'd grown up in small country towns. Opportunity was not far away though, as in 1941 the minimum age to enlist was lowered to 19, with parental permission required for men under 21. On October 13, 1941, at the age of just 19 and five months (and probably accompanied by his mother, who gave her permission), he took his oath and enlisted at Murtoa.

He was assigned to the 7th Battalion, which was an infantry battalion of the Australian Imperial Force made up entirely of Victorian recruits. He began his training on November 5 at Balcombe Training Camp at Mount Martha, on the Mornington Peninsula east of Port Phillip Bay. The camp held up to 3,000 recruits at any one time, and they lived in small tents which they shared with five or six others – unlike the officers who stayed in the more comfortable wooden cabins. Fortunately it was summer time (it was the same warm summer, in fact, that Marge and her siblings were enjoying at Muriel and Fred's farm) so life in a tent could have been worse, although he was the only non-smoker in a tent full of smokers, which he didn't enjoy very much.

Jack was still in Balcombe that December when news came of the Japanese attack on Pearl Harbour, which must have had an enlivening effect on troops eager to march north to defend their homeland. There was worse news to come for Jack though, when he received a telegram notifying him of the death of his mother Kitty on January 29. She was only 46 years old and had been admitted to the Horsham Base Hospital two months before – although she had improved significantly and doctors had been hopeful that she could return home. Sadly, she collapsed unexpectedly one morning and died a week later having never woken up. This must have been a heavy blow for Jack, still a few months shy of his 20th birthday and with four younger siblings still at home – the youngest, June, was only seven. He and his brother Jim both returned to Murtoa for the funeral and, along with their brothers-in-law Fred and Ted and their uncle (Kitty's brother) James McLeod, bore her coffin from her home to the local cemetery, where her many friends and neighbours formed a large gathering at her graveside.

After the funeral Jack was obliged to return to his training camp, though he would not be there for long. At 6 a.m. on Thursday, February 19 – the same day the Japanese launched their bombing attack on Darwin – the most recent graduates of the 7th Battalion marched out from Balcombe to their new posting in the Northern Territory.[*] It was a wet morning, and they waited at an outer suburban station in the pouring rain before boarding their train, and after stopping at Horsham for tea (and to dry off) travelled on to Adelaide. Here the train turned north and carried them through the Flinders Rangers before arriving at Alice Springs on the Monday afternoon, and they were pleased to find everything looking very green after recent showers. They enjoyed their own, much appreciated hot showers before an early start on Tuesday, setting off in a convoy of motor trucks at 4.30 a.m. on an epic 900-mile journey over dirt tracks into the heart of the Northern Territory. They stopped on Thursday evening, and after a 24-hour rest they were bundled into cattle trucks for the last 300

---

[*] Jack and his comrades were among the last recruits to march from the Balcombe Army Camp. Following the Japanese attack on Pearl Harbour at the end of 1941 it was used as a rehabilitation camp for US servicemen and from 1942 it became the headquarters for the 1st division of the US Marine Corps, who used it to practise beach landing exercises with the HMAS Manoora which was moored there. After the war it became the base of the Army Apprentice School.

miles, before arriving at their final destination, teeth rattling and covered in dust, on Saturday evening.

Jack was in the Northern Territory for 18 months as part of several divisions deployed for the defence of Darwin and the coast. The Japanese carried out 64 raids against Darwin and its surrounding bases between February 1942 and November 1943, though none were as deadly or targeted civilians as brazenly as the first. Curiously, Jack was stationed in the Northern Territory at the same time as Robert, although they were not in the same brigade, and considering that battalions were rotated around such a vast area it's unlikely that they would have crossed paths.

Life in the Northern Territory consisted of daily training and drill exercises, patrols and reconnaissance, and for Jack, a trip to the General Hospital in July of 1942 after he developed a carbuncle on his right thigh. A carbuncle is a cluster of boils which forms under the skin, usually caused by a bacterium called Staphylococcus which gets into the skin via a small scratch or wound. On their own, carbuncles are fairly harmless – although highly uncomfortable – and can be treated with warm poultices and antibiotics, but they can be dangerous if the infection spreads to other parts of the body. However, penicillin wouldn't become widely available to the allied forces until 1944, so Jack took a long time to recover and wasn't discharged from the hospital until August 29, almost five weeks later. Fortunately, he was back to normal and able to rejoin his unit by the start of September.

1942 drifted into 1943 and not much changed in the war in the Pacific. Garrison duty and coastal defence may have seemed monotonous at times, but there were diversions to be had too. Athletic tournaments were arranged from time to time, and these included events such as high jump, shot put, discuss, triple jump, relays and even tug-of-war and woodchopping. Cricket and football matches were held regularly, and the troops had a rare opportunity to cheer and chastise their superiors who were brave enough to enter the Officers' 75-Yards Dash.

They received all the usual rations, and soldiers who were felt they needed sprucing up could pay sixpence for a haircut. As Jack didn't drink or smoke he traded his beer and tobacco portions for food and other provisions, perhaps extra stamps for sending letters to his father and siblings, who he must have missed a great deal – they would most certainly have been missing him. On Sundays they were expected to attend services led by the army chaplain and on Christmas Day they were given a special meal of turkey, vegetables and plum pudding, which was served to them at tables by the officers in charge. Each man was also given an extra two bottles of beer, which Jack probably traded for an extra helping or two of plum pudding.

In April 1943 the unit was granted leave to Melbourne and Jack was promoted to Lance-Corporal, the lowest ranking Non-Commissioned Officer. Unlike commissioned officers – such as captains and generals – who gain their commissions from the head of state, NCOs are enlisted members of the forces who gain promotions through the lower ranks, usually to Corporal or Sergeant. NCOs usually received training in management and leadership, and a Lance-Corporal would have served as second-in-command to a small group of soldiers under the supervision of a Corporal. They were responsible for making sure orders were carried out, and were sometimes put in control of the gun group of an infantry section, supervising a small team of up to four soldiers called a fire team, a brick or a crew.

In July the camp was hit by an outbreak of dysentery and several soldiers died, including a Corporal from Jack's unit, Leslie Gange. Jack came through it unscathed, and at the end of the month began a training course at the Northern Territory Force Training School where he spent four weeks attending a Junior Leaders course in drill and weapons training. He passed well, scoring 71% in his written exam, one percent higher than the course average, and an impressive 99% in map reading compared to a course average of 86%. He was graded 'good' for knowledge and bearing and 'very fair' for voice control, and his course leader observed that "this NCO has good knowledge but is too quiet. Needs more drive but should develop into a good leader". While he was there he received the news that his last grandparent, Mary, had passed away in Tasmania at the age of 78, although there was little he could do about it except to send commiserations to his father, who must have felt great affection for the mother who had raised her four children almost on her own. He finished the course on August 31 and rejoined his unit on September 3.

Later that month he returned to Victoria for a few weeks – probably by train – before being sent to Queensland, where he arrived sometime in November. Here the unit underwent intensive pre-deployment training in the Atherton tablelands, including in Canungra. Jack must have impressed his superiors as in March 1944 he was promoted to Acting Corporal, but he only enjoyed his new position for ten days before he was admitted to the 2/2 Australian General Hospital at Rocky Creek near Atherton, this time with an infected hand. He was discharged on March 28 after two weeks of treatment, and a month later was informed that he and his brigade were to be posted to New Guinea.

By this time, the war in the Pacific had been going on for longer than anyone had anticipated, and despite American involvement after the bombing of Pearl Harbour the Japanese had control of most of southern Asia, including Hong Kong, the Philippines, Singapore, Indonesia, Malaysia and Burma. American troops had regained territory in New Guinea, and Australia was now sending troops to support and relieve them.

Jack, along with his comrades of the 7th Battalion, embarked from Cairns on the SS Duntroon on April 24 – the same ship that had transported Robert from Darwin to Cairns less than a year before. They arrived in Lae on the east coast of New Guinea at midnight on May 3 but didn't disembark until the following morning, after which they spent the day setting up camp, putting up tents and familiarizing themselves with their new surroundings.

It wasn't long before they discovered life was a bit different on a tropical island. The next day it rained continuously, so they spent the whole day building roads and drains and clearing mud from the camp. There were thunderstorms all that week, and a landslide blocked a road leading into the camp, necessitating a long diversion for anyone coming in or going out. There were new diseases to contend with, too – malaria was rife and soldiers were ordered not to go out barefoot lest they pick up hookworms, intestinal parasites that live in damp soil and get into the body via the skin.

There were pleasant diversions as well, and the troops were kept fit with regular cricket, football, volleyball and boxing matches. In July the soldiers put on a series of concerts, featuring songs and other performances by members of the troop who may (or may not) have had a talent for entertaining. They gave the shows names like 'Frivolous Frolics' and 'Slim's & Snifters' and amongst the line ups was a ballet featuring Daisy the Cow, a tap dance from a Sergeant J Nicholls and a performance of the Can-Can. Others gave admirable demonstrations on the mouth organ and everyone joined in for rousing renditions of songs like *Oh, Johnny*. There were pictures shown on Wednesday and Saturday evenings at 1845, and they were often entertained with traditional songs and dances from the New Guinean natives who lived alongside the camp. They were allowed to play games in their down time as well, and many of the men learnt to play chess with cardboard sets that had been sent out from home. They were taught, as fate would have it, by the chaplain Cyril Francis, formerly of the 2/13th that was stationed in Tobruk.

Despite not seeing any action in that time, discipline was maintained and morale was good. On August 5 the camp received an inspection from Major General William Bridgeford, commander of the 3rd Infantry Division, and Brigadier Arnold Potts, the initiator of the Queensland jungle training program and the man who'd led the 21st Brigade in the defence of the Kokoda Trail earlier that year. They were happy with what they saw, informing the commanding officers that they were impressed by the cleanliness of the lines and the general fitness of the troops.

Later that year the 7th Battalion would take part in the campaign to take back the Pacific islands from Japan, but Jack would no longer be there – on August 12 he was flown from Nadzab airport near Lae back to Townsville in Queensland to attended another Junior Leaders course. He spent the rest of the year in Queensland, probably training troops coming through the various military programs. On December 12 he was confirmed in the rank of Corporal.

By late 1944 and early 1945 the Allied troops were making headway in the Pacific and fewer reinforcements were needed. At the same time the Australian labour force was experiencing extreme shortages and as a shearer, Jack's skills were now required elsewhere. The 2nd Brigade, of which the 7th Battalion was part, was disbanded on January 8, and Jack was formally discharged from service on February 28, having served 941 days in Australia and 111 abroad. He was still only 22 years old.

In later years he would talk very little about the war and it was clear to his family that he had experienced and witnessed things he preferred not to remember. Much later, he confided to one of his sons that he had done a lot of training with live ammunition, and there had been accidents in which men had been killed – almost certainly his friends and comrades, and quite possibly troops who were under his supervision. He was never court-marshalled, so the incidents – whatever they were – can't have been his fault, but they stayed with him throughout his life and whenever the war was mentioned it cast a shadow over his usually bright features. Like many of the young men who had seen and endured the deprivations of war, he preferred not to talk about it, and his family, in general, left the subject alone.

Jack settled back into civilian life but he didn't stay in Murtoa for long. His father, after having been a widower for just three years had married a Miss Kathleen Callahan, perhaps in the hope that he would have some help with the younger children, or that they would welcome a maternal figure after the loss of their mother. If so he was wrong on both counts – she was not the maternal type and did not wish to have her step children underfoot. The youngest children were sent off to live with their older siblings: Ivan went to Jess and Ted's farm at Kewell, Pat went to her sister May's in Dalmore, south of Melbourne and June went to stay with Jean and her husband Fred, whose eldest daughter Valerie was almost the same age. This sundering of the family had a tremendous impact on the children, particularly for June and Pat who were only 11 and 13 years old and were very close. Not only did it destroy any chances of creating a bond with their stepmother, but it tarnished their relationship with their father as well.

It was at this point that Jack moved to Horsham and he and his brother Jim – who had recently returned from flight training in Canada with his new wife, Eileen – bought a wool and skin shop on Horsham's main street, buying and selling to and from the local farmers. He moved into a boarding home in the town, and that is where he was, early in 1946, when he was asked by a friend of his – remembered only as Hurley – if he could provide a lift for a girl and her friend to a dance he'd invited them to in

Murtoa. Hurley didn't have a car, and the girls lived in Horsham, and as Jack was going to the dance himself it seemed a reasonable arrangement, so he agreed.

Marge, for her part, hadn't been that keen on the dance, or on Hurley for that matter, but her friend wanted to go so she agreed to go too. She climbed into the front of the ute next to Jack, knowing nothing about him other than that he was a friend of Hurley's, and that he had generously agreed to take them to Murtoa and back again, a round trip of roughly an hour. Fortunately they hit it off immediately and they chatted for the entire journey, which seemed to pass much more quickly than they were expecting (although perhaps not for Marge's friend). She was struck by his easy-going manner, and of course she couldn't help noticing how handsome he was! They enjoyed several dances together that night, including the last, much to the annoyance of poor Hurley. The return journey passed just as quickly as the first one, and ended with a promise from Marge to join Jack at the very next dance. Poor Hurley was forgotten, and he never spoke to either of them again.

The months that followed were golden days for Marge, as the absence of her father was forgotten and she got to know her new boyfriend and his very large family. She first met Jim and Eileen and their infant son Glenn, who were lodging with a local woman in Horsham, and the youngest brother, Ivan, who was working for them at the wool shop and boarding in the same house as Jack. His sisters were more spread out, but she was soon on good terms with all of them. Jean, the eldest, was still living in Murtoa with her husband, young children and sister June. The next eldest, Jess, was married and lived on a farm about 15 minutes from Murtoa on the Minyip road, and May was still down in Gippsland with the second youngest, Pat. Mary, who was old enough to work but not yet married, was boarding in Horsham in a house in McPherson Street, and she worked on the telephone exchange with Marge's sister Norma.

Despite being separated the siblings remained close to each other, and when Marge arrived on the scene they accepted her as one of their own. Jean and Jess became like older sisters, June looked up to Marge as another sister and Pat and Mary also became good friends with Shirley, Norma and Freddie. Ivan approved of her as well and encouraged his older brother's relationship, and he was heard more than once to describe her as 'a good sort'.

They were heady days. She and Jack went to all the dances together, and as Jack had a car they were no longer confined to the dances in Horsham. Each evening they piled into the ute – Mary, Pat, Shirley, Norma and their boyfriends in the back, huddled up under their skirts to keep warm, while Marge took the privileged position of front seat inside the ute. They went to dances in Murtoa, Dimboola and other surrounding towns, sometimes three or four nights a week – a fact which Kathleen tolerated as long as they were up and off to work the next morning.

Sometimes Jack took her to the pictures, where he impressed her by buying her boxes of chocolate during the intervals – much better than a single Lion mint! If she was working he sat in the theatre with her, then after the interval they left together to go off to the dances. On the weekends they often went to visit Jean or Jess and their families, and she got on well with Jim and Eileen as well.

Jack also played football for the local team in Horsham, and so Saturdays were often spent at the Horsham oval or at the ground of one of the surrounding townships. When the weather warmed up they resumed their trips out to Green Lake, and sometimes all the way up to the Grampians, now that they had the ute to travel in. Bonny and Eric still rode up on the bike to join them sometimes, and so did Shirley, Norma, Freddie and Jack's younger sisters. Marge didn't mind getting on the bike, although

Jack hated it and would only submit, on rare occasions, to climbing into the sidecar, but Pat in particular loved going out on it. Sometimes four or five of them would be piled on, winding their way up and down the narrow roads and hoping no one was coming the other way.

Kathleen also approved of Jack, and he was often invited round for dinner or lunch on the weekends. He wasn't much of a drinker, which also impressed Kathleen, but just occasionally the boys from the football club would lead him astray and there was one evening when Jack should have turned up after football to take Marge out for the evening. Instead, Marge opened the door to find one of his team mates, looking slightly the worse for wear, explaining that Jack had picked up a bug and would see her tomorrow instead. Marge was not convinced by this story, and sure enough there was Jack the next morning looking very sheepish – not to mention a little green – and promising it wouldn't happen again.

Fortunately he had many good points and it didn't take him long to get into Marge's good books again. He was a keen gardener and helped to set up a vegetable patch for Kathleen, and he made sure to always bring Marge home safely and at a reasonable time. Kathleen always waited up for her, and once she heard the car pull up outside that was the end of the evening – Marge and Jack knew they had a few minutes to say goodnight before she appeared outside banging a saucepan and a wooden spoon, her way of declaring it was time for Marge to come in! At least there weren't too many neighbours around to hear it.

It was a happy time in Marge's life. She had interesting and fulfilling work which she enjoyed, her mother was managing better thanks to the money that she, Shirley and Norma were bringing in, and Bonny was close by so she saw a lot of her young niece Yvonne. But best of all, her evenings and weekends were spent in the company of a young man who enjoyed the same things that she did. He was charming, friendly and polite, and had a large family that felt to Marge like an extension of her own. He had a quick temper, unlike Marge who was inclined to sulk, but it burned off quickly and after a good outburst he was generally back to his normal and contrite self in no time. Like Marge, he was predisposed to enjoy life rather than dwell on past misfortunes, and he had a mischievous streak that appealed to her own sense of adventure. Eventually, to everyone's delight but no one's surprise, he asked her to marry him, and she said yes.

CHAPTER SIX

The First Dance

* * *

The wedding was booked for April 5, 1947, a few weeks before Marge turned 20 and Jack 25. One weekend before the wedding Kathleen hosted a kitchen tea for Marge, and all her sisters and Jack's sisters were there, including Bonny with 7-month-old Yvonne. They were treated to some of Kathleen's famous cakes and biscuits, and each presented Marge with small gifts of things she would need in her new home, including a several kitchen utensils and various bits of linen. Aunty Muriel would also have been there, and family friends from work and church. It must have been a precious moment for Marge, surrounded by her closest friends and family, awaiting the happiest day of her life so far.

The wedding date approached, and plans were made. On the morning of the big day Marge was just getting into her dress when there was a knock on the door – to everyone's horror, it was the groom, who'd come round to ask her about something he was supposed to pack for the honeymoon. The bride's mother and sisters allowed him as far as the bedroom door and he shouted to her from the other side, then made a hasty retreat, much to everyone's relief.

There were no hiccups after that and Marge and her family carried on getting ready. At the time she had a friend who was a dressmaker, and she did all the dresses for the wedding, saving Kathleen a rather large sewing job. By the time they were ready to go they all thought they were looking pretty good – especially Marge, in a dress of tulle over satin, with a bouffant skirt and an embroidered tulle veil. She chose tiger lilies for her bouquet and finished off the outfit with a necklace of pearls, given to her that day as a wedding gift from Jack.

Her bridesmaids were her sisters Shirley and Norma, and Jack's sister Mary, and they wore dresses of lime green taffeta with matching picture hats and bouquets of cactus dahlias and golden gladioli. Since Bonny was married she couldn't be a bridesmaid, but she was there supporting Marge and probably took up her usual job of doing Marge's hair. Kathleen wore a more sombre outfit, a black suit, but dressed it up with London Smoke pink carnations, and Jack's sister Jean, in a smart pink suit with pink tiger lilies, accompanied her through the day. Jack's groomsmen were his brothers Jim and Ivan, and a friend he'd made in the army, Doug Bone.

It was a fine day, and everything went smoothly. The ceremony was conducted at St John's Church of England church in Horsham by the local Reverend Mr Fettell, and as her father was not there she was escorted down the aisle and given away by Uncle Fred, who must have felt immensely proud. She missed her father, but enough time had passed by now and she was used to his not being there, while Fred – who still visited with Muriel every week – felt as much like family as any of their real aunts and uncles did. The service went by smoothly, and they signed the register while a Miss Riley sang the solo *Thanks be to God*. Afterwards the bride and groom, with all their attendants and families, took a short stop at a photographer's studio where they had several family photos taken, including one with all eight of Jack's siblings, in which the twelve-year-old June stood proudly at the front in a new dress. From there they joined the party at the Memorial Hall.

It was a party with all Marge's favourite things – her family, friends, food and dancing. There was plenty to go around, despite rationing still being in place in 1947, as several of Marge's friends had donated their food coupons so she could claim a bit extra. No doubt Kathleen's skills as a cook and in making things go further came to good use again, and the guests would have enjoyed treats of sandwiches, pies, pasties and cakes. There were plenty of children – Yvonne, of course, and all Jack's nieces and nephews – and they sat at their own table enjoying the party in their own way.

In keeping with tradition Marge and Jack opened the festivities with their first dance as husband and wife, which they had no trouble with after all the dances they'd been to together. After that the rest of the bridal party joined in, followed by all the guests, and they danced to all the best tunes from Marge and Jack's courtship. A couple of hours later the bride and groom left to change into their going away outfits, which for Marge was a smart black suit with matching hat and gloves, then returned to the party to say goodbye and for Marge to throw the bouquet. They were due to leave for their honeymoon that evening, but as their train was not leaving until midnight they spent the evening at Kathleen's, along with various family members who were staying in town. This included Jack's father Frederick and some of his uncles – possibly Fred's brother Francis or Kitty's brothers James and David McLeod – who had a jolly time drinking beer and raising glasses to the new couple. Jack didn't join them – he was probably nervous about catching the train on time – and finally they extricated themselves from the revelries and departed Horsham Railway Station as husband and wife.

They honeymooned in Tasmania, which was quite a treat for Marge, as most of the couples she knew hadn't ventured further than other areas of Victoria for their honeymoons. Fortunately for the two of them, Jack had a contact in Tasmania – a man he did business with at the wool shop – so he decided they would go there. It was a special time for Marge. They met Jack's friend and spent a day with him touring his stock rooms and the local market – perhaps not the most romantic day out, but Marge was married to a shearer now and she was keen to learn more about his world. They also toured Port Arthur, the former convict settlement on the southeastern coast of the island which was now a quiet and eerie monument to the colonial era, and visited the Wrest Point Hotel in Hobart, an enormous entertainment complex on the Derwent River estuary which later became Australia's first legal casino. They also found time to attend a ball, and Marge wore a lovely new long frock which her mother had made for her. At the time, Tasmania was the only state to have extended bar closing times to 10 p.m., so they might even have enjoyed a beer or a glass of champagne with their dinner. While they were there they met another young couple also on their honeymoon, but the unlucky groom had managed to break his arm sometime between his wedding and the ball. Jack did the gentlemanly thing and had a couple of dances with the unfortunate bride, but apart from that he and Marge only had eyes for each other, and revelled in the happy days, the long evenings, and the uninterrupted time in the other's company.

It was a perfect honeymoon, spoiled only by the untimely discovery of a certain mischief on the part of Marge's bridesmaids. In those days it was one of the bridesmaid's most important duties to help the bride pack for her honeymoon, and Marge, in her trusting way, had let them get on with it, so didn't discover until she had arrived in their hotel room that they had packed her case full of confetti. It came flying out of her case in an enormous rainbow cloud, covering the floor and every surface in a cascade of coloured dots. Burning with embarrassment, she swept it all under a corner of the carpet and hoped that would be the end of it, but there was no such luck – it stuck to everything and she spent most of the week picking it off her clothes, sweeping it out of the bed and brushing it out of her hair. They had even managed to fill her pockets with it, which she discovered one day when she pulled out a handkerchief and with it came another cloud of confetti! She tucked it away sheepishly, blushing from ear to ear, but thankfully their host at the time had a sense of humour and waved away her apologies. Fortunately for the impish bridesmaids, Marge also had a sense of humour and was too happy to mind too much, so her sisters were forgiven – eventually.

It was a wonderful week and the young couple were gloriously happy in each other's company. But it couldn't last forever, and a week later they were back in Horsham, settling into married life. Jack went back to work at the wool shop, but for Marge, her working days were over – at least for now. Married women didn't work in those days, and so after five years at Coles she had resigned her position to become a full-time housewife. Her manager must have been sorry to lose her – he gave her a glowing reference describing her attendance as good and her ability as outstanding.

For a short time they stayed with Kathleen on Henry Street, and the house was full with Shirley, Norma and Freddie all still living there. Kathleen now had a house full of female boarders as well, including Jack's sister Pat, who was working in Horsham. Marge missed her job at Coles, but at least there was always company at home, and plenty to keep her busy. To start with, there was plenty of housework to help her mother with, and now she was married it was the perfect opportunity for Marge to finally learn how to cook. She joined the Country Women's Association and learned some new crafts – she even made herself a small wooden footstool – and she did get a chance to go back to her old office, not long after she was married, when someone went on holiday for two weeks and they asked her to come back and fill in.

After a few months they got a commission house in Iris Street, just behind Rose Street where Bonny and Eric lived, and she was kept busy settling into her new home. All the gifts and tokens she'd received for her wedding were now put to use, and Jack furnished her with all the appliances she'd need to keep house for him, including a copper for washing clothes, a food safe like her mother's old Coolguardie, and of course a wireless for listening to the news. Her days were filled with cleaning, sewing, knitting, shopping and cooking dinner for the two of them in the evenings. They still had plenty of company with both their families nearby and with Jack still playing football in the winters. He set up a garden with his own fruit trees and vegetables, and eventually they got some chickens so they had a steady supply of fresh eggs, most of which went into cakes and puddings.

There wasn't much time for the dances any more, with a house and husband to look after, but they danced to the wireless in the lounge room and they did occasionally attend a dance or a ball as a special occasion. Sometimes they bumped into Marge's former beau, Jack McCarthy, and the two men exchanged glares and the occasional bump on the dance floor, which caused Marge to smile smugly to herself. They continued going out to visit Jack's family, to Jess and Jean and their families out on their farms. Pat and Mary went with them sometimes, and fortunately Mary was with them on one occasion when the car got stuck, and she and Marge had to get out and push. They managed to get the car out but were splattered all over with mud, and when they arrived Jean went straight into action tidying them up and getting them into clean clothes.

Once a year in November they travelled to Maryborough for Jack's army reunion, and while they were there they always took the time to visit Marge's grandfather Walter. These trips were always good fun for both of them and Walter must have enjoyed them too – as Robert was his only child and was still nowhere to be found, Marge and her siblings were his only descendants. Walter had lived most of his life in Maryborough, where his parents had been amongst the town's first settlers, lured from England by the discovery of gold in the area. His father, Edward, established a hardware and tinsmithing business in the high street of the town and enjoyed a very successful trade supplying lamps, billy cans and tin bowls to the gold mines. Later he expanded into water tanks, which he sold throughout Victoria, and subsequently he and his wife Eliza were among the town's most prosperous residents. Eliza, Walter's mother, was one of the leading ladies in Maryborough's social circles, and was a prominent figure in the Ladies Benevolent Society – a charity helping the old and infirm in the days before pensions and social security.

Walter was one of several children, including five boys of which he was the only one who didn't follow his father into the ironmongery business. Instead, shortly after he married Georgina and their son Robert was born, they moved to North Brighton where he bought the store where Robert would later work as an assistant. Some years later he returned to Maryborough a widower, where he took over the running of a large garden owned by the family on the corner of Inkerman and Goldsmith Streets. It had been previously used to grow fruit and vegetables, had housed chickens and even the family cow at one point, but Walter used it to grow gladioli. Each morning he took fresh flowers to sell at the local market, then he bought his milk, meat and bread for the day before heading home. He married Janet in 1936 at the age of 65.

He enjoyed having visitors, including his grandchildren, who always enjoyed looking through his collections of stamps, matchboxes and fruit tin labels. He insisted on doing all the cooking whenever he had visitors, enjoying company in the kitchen for breakfast and lunch but always serving a proper meal in the dining room for dinner. After that he would sit back, moustache bristling and waistcoat straining over his large frame, to enjoy a chat and pipe or two in the evening.

Walter and Jack always got on well, probably because they were both so passionate about gardens and agriculture. Walter had been made secretary of the local Agricultural Society when he had returned to Maryborough, and he spent many hours working at the showground on its behalf – he even became known as 'Mr Society'. He and Jack had similar temperaments too, it seemed, as Walter was just as hot tempered and likely to boil over at the slightest provocation. One of his fellow society members offended him so much on one occasion that he stormed out of the meeting threatening to resign his position. He was discovered a couple of hours later, his jacket slung over the wall of a barn, shovelling furiously to 'let off steam'. Needless to say, he was perfectly fine after that and didn't resign from the society.

Sometime early in 1948 came the exciting news that Marge was expecting a child. Now she was busier than ever, getting the house ready and knitting clothes for the baby. They were in for more big news, however, when at about seven months the doctors suspected she might be carrying twins, and sent her for an x-ray which confirmed it. She doubled her efforts, making and knitting two of everything – but despite being busy she was happier than ever and full of excitement at the prospect of being a mother.

She had regular check-ups and at one point developed some kidney trouble, so the doctor put her on a diet of lamb's fry, tripe and brains – fortunately, they were all things that she liked. She sat on the little wooden stool that she had made herself while she was chopping and peeling vegetables, and she was told to rest as much as possible – which for Marge, was not very much! Fortunately, the kidney trouble cleared up and there were no more complications.

October arrived and they waited for the babies to come any day now. A week went by, and another, and it appeared the babies would be taking their time. It was the beginning of November when the big day finally arrived, by which time she was three weeks overdue. She arrived at the labour ward at the hospital in Horsham and was given over to the care of a Matron Arthur. As it was her first pregnancy – and twins – the nurses expected that it would be a long labour, and told her not to fret but to relax, as it would be a while before anything happened. A caesarean was not considered, despite the fact that she was carrying twins and was so overdue – it was still a fairly new procedure in the 1940s, with only 2% of babies delivered that way, and the survival rate was very low. Instead, they gave her a cup of castor oil to drink, which was a common practice then, as it was believed that the castor oil would stimulate the gut, which in turn would stimulate the womb and induce labour (several studies have been done on the effectiveness of this treatment, and none have been able to prove anything other than its efficacy as a laxative). Not knowing any better, she accepted the castor oil and of course thought it was disgusting. She was in for a few more shocks too: in those days, very little information was given to expectant mothers about what birth would actually be like, and although Bonny could have told her something about it, there was still an amount of taboo around the subject, so when the pains started much earlier than anyone expected, and she found herself being strapped to a bed and wheeled into a delivery room, the 21-year-old Marge found it all a bit terrifying.

The first baby was a boy, born on November 2, and they called him Ronald. He came relatively easily, and they all expected the second baby to follow shortly afterwards. Unfortunately it was not to be. It had become stuck, and labour dragged on into the following day. Several doctors were called in to look at her, and they tried strapping her up one way and then another, each one trying a different method, but nothing helped. By now Marge was exhausted and in terrible pain, despite pain killers such as gas and pethidine being available. Jack was not permitted to be in the delivery room, but in the circumstances they did let him in to see her from time to time – not that she was aware of it. He spent the rest of the time patrolling the corridors outside in a state of high anxiety and napping in a chair when he could. The baby Ron was placed in the care of hospital nurses for the time being, and no doubt his grandmother and numerous aunts were on hand to help.

Matron Arthur remained by Marge's side, sponging her face, brushing her hair and offering reassurance, and her presence was a comfort to Marge even in her drug-induced state. Eventually they managed to turn the baby around and get it out, two days after Ron had come so easily. It was a girl, and she was stillborn.

Delivery was finally over, but Marge was not out of danger. Two days of labour had brought her to the point of exhaustion, and a fever was setting in. Doctors suspected septicaemia, which in the 1940s and coupled with her weak state was a potentially deadly situation. The doctors would have had to warn Jack to prepare for the worst.*

Fortunately by that time antibiotics such as penicillin and sulphonamides had become available, but doctors still feared for her life so she was moved to intensive care, where the indomitable Matron Arthur kept her under a 24-hour watch.** The nurses and sisters took good care of her, changing her nightgowns several times as they became soaked with sweat, but exhausted as she was and delirious with fever, Marge barely noticed.

---

* It was not uncommon in the 1940s for a second twin to get into trouble, especially if it was a breech presentation. Unfortunately the medical records no longer survive, but the earlier kidney trouble, added to fact that it was a multiple first pregnancy, makes it very likely that she was suffering from pre and postpartum eclampsia (also known as toxaemia), a rare condition characterised by high blood pressure and severe headaches. In the 1940s postpartum eclampsia had a death rate of around 13%. The septicaemia was probably caused by having ruptured membranes for such an extended time.

** A few years later Matron Arthur retired after 24 years at the Wimmera Base Hospital. In her honour, a new street in Horsham was named Arthur Street, and at a special luncheon of the Past Trainees' Association of the Wimmera Base Hospital she was presented with retirement gifts of a wallet of notes, several pairs of stockings and an electric stovette. The Wimmera Care Group now incorporates the Matron Arthur Manor, part of the Wimmera Nursing Home.

Meanwhile, the stillborn baby girl had been taken away and buried in a quiet ceremony with only a priest, Jack and his brother Jim present. Marge was never allowed to see her.

On the second day after the birth Marge began to recover, and by the third day she was well enough to get out of bed. She was moved out of intensive care and into a ward, where she spent another week recovering and learning to look after Ron, and it seemed to Marge like an endless cycle of crying, feeding and sleeping. There had been no classes or books or anything to teach her what to expect, so she had to learn everything as she went, from bathing and dressing to feeding and changing. It was a lot to take in all at once, especially as she was still recovering from the traumatic and exhausting delivery, and it was a steep learning curve. She had many visitors, each with their own different advice, and it was hard not to feel overwhelmed. Eventually she got the hang of it, of course, but she tended to agree with her sister-in-law Eileen who observed, 'it's a wonder the first one ever survives'.

Finally, after almost two weeks in hospital, doctors declared her fully recovered and she was ready to go home and start her new life as a mother. This was a time of mixed emotions for Marge, as she dealt with the fatigue left over from her long delivery, her joy at having the baby Ron, and her terrible grief at losing his twin. After months of expecting two babies, arriving at home with only one was both a happy and a sad occasion. Naturally they had prepared to welcome two babies, and so there waiting for her when she got home were two sets of clothes, two bottles, two piles of nappies, and two cots, and everywhere she turned it seemed there was something to remind her of what she had lost.

There were no grief counselling services in those days, and it was generally accepted that the best way to deal with this kind of trauma was not to talk about it, but to forget about it and move on. This was easier said than done, and it certainly didn't help when people offered advice along the lines of 'well at least you've still got one baby', and it took all her restraint not to tell these people what she really thought of their advice. The one baby, on the other hand, had no idea of the events succeeding his birth and was as demanding as any new baby can be. He couldn't take away their sadness, but at least he did give Marge a purpose and routine. She had to get up, she had to tend to him, and she had to keep house for Jack, who'd gone back to work. She fed the baby, she washed his nappies and she cooked dinner in the evenings. She kept going, because that was all she could do, and despite her grief, she loved Ron with all her heart.

She also had the support of her family, and her mother and sisters were never far away. Jack was there, and he shared her sadness. They tried to discuss what had happened, but they didn't know what to do about it, and there was no one they could ask. Eventually they found they had stopped talking about it, and life moved on.

As for being a father, Jack revelled in it and loved his son more than anything he'd had before. He'd been reluctant, at the beginning of their marriage, to consider having children, probably because of the upheaval and anguish experienced by his own family when his mother had died young and his younger siblings had been sent away. Now that he found himself with a son of his own, however, he was as proud as any new father can be and willing to help as much as he could. Any noise, any gurgle or cry in the night and he was up, first to his side, and if he couldn't get him to settle down he popped him into the car seat and drove him around the neighbourhood until he was asleep again. He tidied up the garden so it was safe for the baby, and they spent many afternoons and evenings outside on the lawn as the nights got warmer and the days grew longer, and Marge watched as he played with his son and chatted to him as he tended the vegetables.

December came, and Ron's first Christmas. They spent it as usual at

Kathleen's with all the family, and she made her traditional roast turkey and pork with all the trimmings, followed by her famous plum pudding. Gifts were small but lovingly made – aprons, handkerchiefs or potholders, for example, and Marge always knitted jumpers for the children.

Time passed, and they healed, and life settled into a pleasant routine. Jack was still working at the wool shop, and loved it, and Marge got better and better at being a mum. She visited the local clinic regularly, where the baby was checked over and weighed and they could offer advice if she was having any difficulties. The nurses could be stern but were very efficient – they gave her tips for getting the nappies on and off and insisted they stay off while he was weighed, resulting in many unpleasant sprinkles.

They were full of advice, some of which Marge found hard to follow (she hated letting him cry) but there was one thing she was grateful for their help with. Ron was proving to be a tricky feeder at first, probably a result of having spent his first few days being bottle-fed by nurses, and it took him a while to get used to breastfeeding. Marge was nervous and uptight about it as well, and in those days nurses insisted that babies should be breast fed. Fortunately Ron was a hungry baby and he did get used to it, much to everyone's relief.

The clinics were a great support to Marge, and everything was recorded in a book for her to keep. She also joined a local mother's group, which met regularly to have tea and talk about the babies. She enjoyed the company as well as the support, not to mention a receptive audience when it came to talking about Ron's latest accomplishment or her own achievements. Being able to share her worries and concerns was a great comfort as well.

Sometimes they took the baby for a walk to visit Bonny or Kathleen, and at other times Yvonne, now a toddler with an apparently healthy independent streak, would vanish from home to be found at her Aunty Marge's, doting over her baby cousin. There were always fetes and markets being held at the school or church hall, and on these occasions Kathleen was busy for days beforehand, cooking up trays of toffees, marshmallows and coconut ices. She won many awards for her cooking, and no doubt her grandchildren were on hand to test each batch and make sure it was up to standard.

On Sundays they all met at church, where Ron was christened, and Kathleen joined them, dressed in her Sunday best and ready to take Yvonne and her new sister Kathleen, named for her grandmother, in to Sunday School. After church Marge, Jack, Bonny, Eric and the children all went round to Kathleen's to enjoy one of her special roast dinners, followed by a sponge pudding with generous dollops of cream. Jack kept her garden tended for her, and she in turn doted on her grandchildren and was always happy to babysit if Marge and Jack had a wedding or ball to go to. The children always loved going to Grandma's house, although 'Grandma' was too much of a mouthful for young Yvonne at that age, so she just called her Gar, which somehow stuck. The family grew, as Marge and Jack's younger siblings grew up and got married, so there was always another niece or nephew on the way. There were Christmases, New Years, birthdays, weddings, christenings and confirmations, and they were always celebrated at Gar's house. She was the heart of her big family, the one constant in their changing lives, and now that Marge was a mother herself, she appreciated her more than ever.

CHAPTER SEVEN

Click go the Shears

***

The early years of Marge and Jack's marriage were simple but good. They didn't go out on their own much, and they didn't have many treats, but life was full and they didn't miss what they couldn't afford. Jack was drawing in five pounds a week – slightly less than the average factory worker's wage and equivalent to about $300 today. After taking out rent, groceries and expenses for the baby there wasn't much left over, but they grew a lot of their own food, they had their own eggs, Kathleen helped with clothes and Marge, of course, was always knitting. For Ron, there were plenty of hand-me-downs from his cousins, and nappies were always washed and reused. They never ate out, except to visit their friends and family, but sometimes – when they could afford it – Jack might buy a bottle of beer to enjoy in his garden, or in his chair by the fire in the winter.

Jack was still a member of the Horsham Football Club and played in the winter months, and Marge took the baby to watch when she could. She remained a member of the CWA, and she went to meetings with her mother and Aunty Muriel where she honed her skills in crafts and sewing. But her favourite craft was knitting, and in the evenings, after an early dinner, she and Jack sat together and listened to the wireless, chatting and winding down to the steady clicking of knitting needles.

They saw a lot of Jack's family too and went to visit Frederick and his second wife Kathleen in Murtoa from time to time. Marge found Frederick a little old fashioned, but he was a caring grandfather who enjoyed playing with his grandchildren, and when each one was born he presented them with two shillings for prosperity. Kathleen, despite being despised by most of her stepchildren, was always polite to Marge, and they harboured no particular ill-feelings towards her, so the visits were pleasant enough.

They didn't go on many holidays, but they had a tiny caravan which they used to visit relatives living further afield. Once, they volunteered to help Jack's sister Jess and her husband Ted by looking after their farm for a week, although tending to livestock wasn't exactly Marge's idea of a break – especially when the farmhouse was overrun by mice and it was all she could do to keep herself and the baby off the floor until Jack arrived to rescue them.

Occasionally the local farmers put on a big dance in one of the shearing sheds, and they always looked forward to a chance to dress up and dust off their dancing shoes. One of their favourites was a big annual event put on by the parents of Jack's army mate Roger, and the huge shed was cleared and set up with hay bales all around it for people to sit on. There was always a big band and they danced all night, stopping only for supper and to tend the baby – though there were plenty of volunteers to look after him. These events were a chance to relax with the other farmers and shearers away from the heat and stress of the shearing sheds and on one occasion Jack even took the chance to enjoy a few beers, something he didn't do very often. Unluckily, this resulted in an accident coming home when he drove the car into a tree – fortunately he wasn't going very fast at the time and one of the front tyres bore most of the damage. There were lots of other cars going home that way and it wasn't long before someone stopped to help, but Jack was terribly upset that such a thing had happened with his wife and child in the car, and he made sure he never did it again.

When Ron was nine months old Marge began feeding him solid foods, which is what the nurses recommended in those days. She started him off on Milk Arrowroot biscuits, which she softened by pouring boiling water over them and then milk, and perhaps a bit of sugar. She did the same with Weet-Bix, and gradually moved him on to soft vegetables and fruit. He grew quickly and loved to play outside, and it wasn't long before Jack was teaching him to kick a football. He also had an uncanny knack for fixing things, which had some interesting results when combined with a child's logic – for instance, he noticed at his grandmother's house that people were always having to open and close the door to get in and out, which was obviously a terrible inconvenience. He solved the problem by removing all the hinges from the door, so that when the next person pushed it open it fell through and hit the floor with a resounding crash. Though his parents shook their heads in exasperation, the young Ron felt pretty pleased with himself for having solved such a consistent problem.

As the 1940s drew to a close, changes were coming for Marge and Jack. Jim was growing restless and wanted to move on from the wool shop, but this meant that Jack, who couldn't afford to buy his brother's share, was forced to sell too. They sold the shop and Jack fell back on his old career as a shearer, taking work on farms in the surrounding areas. He was good at the job, but the work was naturally limited by the amount of sheep on each farm. He had to take work further and further afield, and sometimes this meant staying away from home – often on weekends as well. He always came home if he could, but Marge was now on her own for most of the week, which she didn't mind as long as money was coming in, but she missed his company despite having plenty of family still around.

She did have a chance to go with him on one occasion, however, when she received an SOS from the farm he had just arrived at saying the regular cook hadn't turned up, and could she fill in for the week. She agreed, despite being terrified at the prospect, and so she packed up herself and Ron into the van and they followed Jack out into the bush.

It was a demanding week. Each morning she was up early to have breakfast ready for the shearers by 6:30, usually sausages or chops and eggs. At 10:30 she served them a morning tea of biscuits, cake or scones, and lunch was cold meat or sandwiches, depending on what was left over. They stopped again for afternoon tea, and then finished with a hot meal at night, usually roast lamb or a lamb stew. It was quite a challenge for someone who didn't like cooking, but fortunately the cook who hadn't turned up had already ordered the supplies, so she had plenty of potatoes and veggies to work with and there was a fresh supply of bread delivered each day. Jack helped her cut up the lamb from the joint, and there was always someone on hand to help with the washing up. As long as the men had three good meals a day they were happy, and were especially appreciative of her sausage rolls, which she made with lamb because that was all she had. She made some good money, but she was happy when the week was done and she and Ron could return home.

In 1950 there was some excitement in Horsham as the town was celebrating its centenary. A week of events was planned for the first week in October to coincide with the annual agricultural show, which was opened by the governor, Sir Dallas Brooks. People poured in from the surrounding areas to join in the festivities, which began with a procession of floats including St George and the Dragon and an old wagon pulled by a bullock team. Citizens were encouraged to attend balls and dances in fancy dress, and arrangements included a teenagers' dance, a women's only reception at the town hall and an old folks' tea. For entertainment, children performed a maypole dance, there was a concert from the Victorian Police Highland Pipe Band and an air show by the RAAF, but for many the highlight was the agricultural show which enjoyed a record-breaking attendance of 20,000 on its first day. Every night parties and carnivals were held in the streets, which were decorated with miles of bunting and special lighting.

Once the party mood had settled life moved along into a new decade, and with it came big changes. In the 1950s, the western world was experiencing a post-war boom – marriage and birth rates soared, an influx of European immigrants brought a much-needed boost to the working population of Australia, and new suburbs sprang up in every major city, full of large, detached houses each on their own even larger block of land. Employment was high, and the number of women in universities and in the workforce was rising. Around the world, money was being invested in new technologies and advances were being made in electronics and circuitry that would pave the way for modern living and the beginning of the space age. Progress in medicine and science was improving the quality of living all the time and Rock'n'roll burst on to the music scene, bringing with it a new generation of artists like Chuck Berry, Elvis and the Beatles, which would go on to reinvent old concepts of celebrity and facilitate the emergence of a new teenage identity (much to their parents' concern and disapproval).

And yet, as some parts of the world were zooming forwards, others were stagnating and some were hurtling backwards at an alarming pace. In the United States, the civil rights movement – which would bring an end to segregation – was just kicking off, but at the same time Apartheid was only beginning to take hold in South Africa. In just a few months' time, North

Korea would invade South Korea, sparking a war that would last three years and involve six million soldiers from 25 different nations. By the end of the decade the Americans would be fully committed to the conflict in Vietnam and the Cold War would have the world sitting on a knife's edge, with nuclear winter a fearsome possibility. In many ways, the fifties would be an era of extremes, but at the beginning of 1950 all that was to come and for now, at least, the future seemed bright – the next generation looked forward with optimism to a new world full of opportunity.

Closer to home, more changes were coming for Marge and Jack, too. In the second half of 1951 Marge discovered that she was pregnant again, and some new plans had to be made. Together she and Jack made the decision to travel north towards Mildura, where there were bigger sheep stations and he would be able to find more work. They bought a new and bigger caravan, and began packing up the house, so that in the final weeks of Marge's pregnancy they were just about ready to go. Once again, it seemed to drag on and on, and Jack, who was fortunately working close by in Murtoa at that time, returned every day to find an exhausted Marge fed up almost to the point of tears, and not particularly receptive when he joked that she was 'still here then?'

At last, at the end of March, the day arrived and she went to hospital where a daughter, named Katherine after Jack's mother, was born on the 31st. Marge was monitored carefully, given the difficulties of her previous delivery, but there were no complications this time and after her ten days in hospital she was declared fit for discharge and allowed to go home. Within a few days of that they finished emptying the house, hitched the caravan on to the back of the car and headed north, with three-year-old Ron sitting on own his own in the back and Marge in the front, holding the baby on a cushion on her lap.

They spent the rest of 1952 moving around in the caravan from one sheep station to another, in the area around Mildura in rural Victoria and New South Wales. They lived in the van on remote farms and homesteads, sometimes more than a hundred kilometres away from any town or settlement. They had basic facilities and limited communication, but they discovered a new lifestyle and a freedom of movement which they loved. There were several other shearers, also with their wives and families, so they became a kind of travelling community, moving from one station to another as the work demanded.

Gradually they settled into a new kind of routine. Jack rose early to join the other shearers for breakfast before starting work, and he took his evening meal with them before heading back to the van and going to bed early after a hard day. As a result, Marge didn't see much of him during the week, but he was around on weekends – though as there were no towns for miles around and he was always tired after a hard week, they didn't do much. Sometimes the farmers put on a dance for them in one of the shearing sheds, and Marge and Jack always looked forward to dressing up and going out, even if it was only across the field. On Sundays they slept in if they could, and enjoyed playing games, perhaps cards, dominoes or Chinese Checkers, and they listened to the wireless when they weren't too far out and could pick up a signal. Marge, of course, had her knitting, and she carried on making jumpers, hats and scarves whenever she had supplies.

She also had a sewing machine with her, which she used when she had to. She didn't enjoy sewing as much as she loved knitting, and she was never as good as her mother, but necessity dictated that she had to learn, and she made shirts, shorts and trousers for the children, and mended whatever needed mending. She also had to adjust and mend clothes for Jack, who needed particular clothes for working in.

The shearers wore flannel shirts to absorb perspiration and denim pants for durability. Marge would alter the shirts by sewing a large patch of heavy calico from the front to half way round the back, to protect it where it was held against the sheep. The trousers were a bit more fiddly, as she had to undo the inside leg, add a heavy patch to reinforce it and then do up the seam again – not an ideal job for someone who hated sewing, but it had to be done, so she didn't complain. She then had the unpleasant job of washing his clothes after he'd been working in the hot shed all day.

Despite being manual work, shearing a sheep is a practised art. Depending on the breed, an adult female can weigh up to 100kg and although they always feel better after being shorn, they don't like the process very much and can kick hard. To keep a sheep still, the shearer had to hold its head between his legs, facing forward, and stand with one leg on either side of it to stop it from kicking. At the beginning of each day all the sheep were rounded up into individual catching pens – one for each shearer – and as each sheep was finished it was pushed into another letting out pen as the shearer reached for another one. Jack and his colleagues were paid for the number of sheep shorn, so they learned to work very fast, but still with enough precision to preserve the quality of the wool and not harm the sheep. At the end of each day the sheep were released and counted, and the top shearer was called the ringer.

Jack found the work hard but satisfying, and life in the shearing shed was fast-paced but organised. In the 1950s Australia was the world's biggest exporter of wool, so it was important work and farmers invested a great deal of money and resources into their product. Each station could have anywhere from a few hundred to a few thousand sheep, and with the new mechanical shears that were becoming more widely used, a good shearer could manage between one and two hundred a day. Some shearers, who had been around for a long time, could do between 200 and 400 sheep a day, and they were known as gun shearers.

A practiced shearer could get an entire fleece off in one piece, but it took years of practice and even the best sometimes nicked the skin, and then it was the job of the roustabout to run over with the tar and patch it up. Once the sheep was shorn, the roustabout had to gather up the fleece as fast as he could and throw it over a table to be classed and trimmed. Here the wool picker, under the supervision of the wool classer, pulled off any bits that were stained with blood, sweat or excrement, or contained bits of grass or skin (a process known as skirting) and these went into separate bins for cleaning and sorting later. The finer wool from the face, neck and belly was also separated, then the rest was classed and graded depending on quality and size and put into a respective bin, to be pressed into a bundle for sale. Meanwhile the roustabout had to run back and sweep the board – the wooden floor that the shearers worked on, kept smooth and polished so the sheep would slide easily on it – so the shearer could start on the next sheep. All this would happen in a matter of minutes, before the next fleece was ready to be picked up – a roustabout was never still for long.

Once the wool was in the pressing machine, the presser – yet another worker who operated the machine – compressed the wool into bales weighing up to 170kg, which were bound in hessian sacks and loaded up on to trucks. It was hard work, and they started early, taking breaks throughout the day. Sometimes there was time for a nap, and Jack developed an extraordinary ability to lie down and sleep on any surface and wake up after exactly ten minutes as fresh and ready to work again as if he'd had a full night's sleep. Others were tempted to take a nap in the wool presser, where the wool was still soft and warm from the sheep, but this was discouraged because they sometimes didn't wake up when the machine was turned on, and if the operator didn't know they were in there they would go ahead and press the bale, suffocating the man inside. Only later, when a man was noticed missing, would they open the bale and find him, too late to do anything about it.

Stories like that were uncommon but they did happen, and a report may have reached them in September that year of the tragic death of 18-month-old Gerrard Brady. Gerrard had wandered into his family's woolshed in Ararat and his father had placed him in the empty wool presser to keep him out of the way. Mr Brady was then called away before he could tell anyone, and in the meantime his brother started up the machine, not knowing that his nephew was inside.

At the end of the day, the men took their evening meal together and perhaps enjoyed a quiet beer or cigarette and a yarn or two. Then they'd have just enough energy left in the evenings to shower, kiss their wives goodnight and go to bed.

It was a different sort of life, but a peaceful one. For Marge, it was the first time in her twenty five years she had lived away from her family and she missed them dearly, but she loved living close to the land, where the sounds of a busy town were replaced with the calls of the birds, the wind whistling in the gum trees and the gentle but constant hum of farm machinery. She spent her days looking after the children and keeping house in a different way, cooking meals for the three of them and keeping the caravan clean and tidy. With a baby and a toddler there were always clothes, sheets and nappies to wash, which she hung up on lines around the farm, or strung from one van to another to dry.

The van was small – the children shared a bed on one side and Marge and Jack slept on the other – with a small kitchen and table in the middle. They had kerosene lights but no heating, although the climate in northern Victoria was mild and dry so this wasn't an issue for most of the year, and in winter they lit campfires to sit around in the evenings. It rained occasionally, but fortunately their caravan was new and therefore fairly weatherproof.

One other couple was not so lucky – after one memorable trip to the next farm, travelling in convoy through heavy, persistent rain, they found that mud had come up through the bottom of the van and every surface was covered, including the inside of every drawer and cupboard.

The caravans didn't have bathroom facilities, but the farms had long drop toilets and the women were allowed to use the men's showers during the day, so they took the children over in the afternoons for their baths, and to do the washing while the men were working. The farmers' wives were always very welcoming, and sent over meat and milk for the children, and Marge became particularly good at cooking lamb. The farms kept them well stocked with vegetables too, so despite the lack of variety their diet was a balanced one.

In time Marge learned to love living out in the bush, the open spaces, the quiet and the company of the other families. Katherine was still a baby, but she ate and slept well and was easy to care for. Ron was a curious but well-behaved child, which was fortunate as in many places he was the only child there, and he was quite good at entertaining himself. He particularly loved to watch the men as they worked, and as long as he wasn't underfoot the men didn't mind him being there. He was particularly fascinated by anything to do with machinery, and he was often to be found perched on a hay bale in the corner of the shearing shed, quietly observing everything that was going on. It only happened once that he fell asleep in the wool presser, but fortunately the operator spotted him before he turned it on. He even managed to save the pressing machine once, when he noticed the operator was about to start it with the safety pins still in. The man was just about to pull the lever when a small voice from the corner peeped, "you haven't taken the pins out!". He probably felt a bit sheepish, but was grateful enough to tell Marge about it later.

Sometimes there were other children, and Ron enjoyed having company.

There were balls to play with, and the whole campsite to explore, and as there were no roads, or in fact anything at all, for miles around, they were generally told to stay within sight and then left to themselves. It only went wrong once when a young girl about Ron's age picked up a tin of kerosene that had been left at the back of a van and drank it. The alarm was sounded, but no one knew what to do, so she was rushed to hospital, miles away across paddocks and paddocks of closed gates. Those with cars rushed ahead to open the gates in advance, and thankfully and they made it in time to save her. Everyone was a bit more careful after that.

The shearing season carried on through the autumn and into July, and they stayed on each station for about ten days or so before moving on. There was still plenty of work in the winter months, as many farmers hired shearers for a procedure known as crutching. This involved shearing the wool from around the animals' back legs and hindquarters, which helped to prevent a condition known as flystrike – an infestation of fly larvae (or maggots) – which was common in excrement-soaked wool. Crutching also helped to keep the rest of the fleece clean, and depending on the weather or the condition of the rest of the fleece, the farmer might also ask them to shear the underbelly and face to stop the animal collecting seeds and mud when the fields were damp.

Life on the road was different, but there was work all year round and what they lacked in security they gained in freedom and the companionship of the other families. At the end of the first year they returned to Horsham for Christmas, and then they started the whole cycle again, returning to many of the same farms in the new year. Most of the other shearers returned as well, and once again they travelled together so that they became a sort of extended family, ready to lend a hand if anyone needed help or broke down. The farmers were always pleased to see them, and so were their wives, who didn't get much company living in such remote places and loved having the children around. Marge often joined them in the farm kitchens at lunch time, helping wash up after the men had eaten while Ron sat and watched quietly.

They spent a second winter on the road, but once again changes were coming and life was about to force them in a new direction. Ron was approaching his fifth birthday and would need to start school the next year, and very soon they would find their small caravan becoming uncomfortably crowded, because Marge was pregnant again.

CHAPTER EIGHT

The 1950s Housewife

* * *

By October of 1953, Marge and Jack had sold the caravan and settled in Mildura. Jim and Eileen were already living there on 12th Street, so they bought a house just a couple of streets away on Sarnia Avenue. It was lovely to have their own home, after more than a year of living in the van, and Ron loved being close to his cousins Glenn and Wayne. The two houses backed onto the same small lane, and the three of them were often to be found heading out of one back gate and into the other. By this time Jack's father, Frederick, who was now known to everyone as 'Silver', had also moved to Mildura and was living in a small flat at the back of Jim and Eileen's property, so despite the fact that Marge was once again a newcomer in a strange town, there were familiar faces around her.

She busied herself with setting up her new home and getting ready for the new baby. It was a small house with only two bedrooms, but at least it was bigger than a caravan, and it had more modern amenities – including electric light. Unfortunately it didn't have a flushing toilet, as it wasn't connected to the town's sewerage, so instead they had a large galvanised iron pan out in the back yard which everything got emptied into. This was Jack's job, unless he was away, when the job fell to Ron, who took it on with all the aplomb he could muster. Once a week the dunnyman called round, accessing the garden via the lane at the back. He came through the gate in a full leather suit, hoisted the pan up onto his shoulder with a well-practised manoeuvre and carried it out to his truck to empty it.

Being in a town also meant that the children could have birthday parties again, and so on Saturday the 31st October – two days before Ron's 5th birthday – Marge invited their cousins and some friends around for a party. It was destined to be interrupted though, as Ron's unborn sibling was apparently ready to join in. Marge was rushed off to hospital, leaving Eileen and Kathleen, who'd come to stay, to look after the children, and not long afterwards into the world came Gregory Arthur, a third child for Marge and Jack and a younger brother for Ron and Katherine.

They soon settled into life in Mildura. Jack continued taking shearing jobs, which meant that he was away most weeks, but he always came home on weekends if he could. In the summer months he had to travel further afield, sometimes all the way over to Tasmania, but he was always home in time for Christmas, which they shared with Jim and Eileen. He wasn't much of a handyman, but as usual he was keen to get the garden going and it wasn't long before Marge had home grown fruit and vegetables to cook. He bought them some chickens too, so they had fresh eggs every day to eat or bake with.

In January 1954 Ron started school, and as it was only one street away it wasn't long before he was able to walk there on his own or with his cousins. Marge was busier than ever at home, as there was no kindergarten in town where she could send the younger children. Taking matters into their own hands, she and a group of mothers from the church banded together to start fundraising, knitting, sewing and baking at all hours of the day and night so they could sell their creations at fetes and markets. Their hard work paid off and eventually the new kindergarten was opened, and Katherine was among its first pupils.

Despite having the children out of the way at kindy, Marge still had plenty to do at home. On Mondays she did the washing, boiling everything up in an old copper just as her mother used to do. First, she had to get the fire going, and then sheets, clothes and linen all went in with shavings of velvet soap cut off a larger block. There wasn't any antiseptic in those days, so everything had to boil for an hour or two to kill any germs. Then everything had to be rinsed and pulled through the mangle, then rinsed again with a blue rinse added to counteract any yellowing or greying. After a final squeeze through the mangle it was hung up to dry, which was the most back-breaking step of the whole process. It was fascinating for the children, especially for the boys who were forever trying to get their sister into trouble. One day they persuaded Katherine to see how far she could get her arm into the mangle, and inevitably she got stuck and had to be cut out, which meant an extra dreaded sewing job for Marge.

On Tuesdays Marge did the ironing, using a flat iron heated on the stove, and of course there were always nappies to wash. She soaked a new batch each day, and on Mondays they went through the wash with everything else. She cooked for them all every evening, and as usual the thing she cooked most often was lamb. She made lamb stew, lamb chops, lamb cutlets and lamb casseroles, all with Jack's home-grown vegetables of course. When there wasn't lamb she boiled up a joint of mutton and though the children grew weary of eating the same thing all the time, at least they didn't go hungry. The farms and farmers that Jack worked for kept them well supplied, and gradually Marge's repertoire expanded, with recipes she picked up from her friends and in magazines. She made soups too, especially when anyone was unwell, and when Jack's youngest sister June, who was living with Jim and Eileen for a little while, became sick with yellow jaundice, Marge turned up with an enormous bowl of homemade soup – a gesture which bolstered June's spirits as well as her health.

In the 1950s the Australian diet was very much of the 'meat and three veg' kind. Fresh ingredients were all home grown or bought locally, and the influence of European and Asian migrants on food and cooking had yet to take hold. Stews and casseroles with beef, lamb or sausages still featured heavily, especially in winter, and for dessert apple crumbles, rice puddings and roly polys were the staples of every housewife's repertoire. Mint and parsley were the most popular herbs, and if there was a salad, it was served as a side, not as the meal itself. Potatoes, pumpkins, peas, carrots and beans were still the most common vegetables, but tomatoes, silverbeet and leeks were becoming more popular with home growers. The Australian Women's Weekly had always been the 1950s housewife's go-to authority on sewing and knitting patterns, but now it was branching out to cooking and baking, and with the rise in popularity of dinner parties and backyard entertaining its pages now featured such fashionable treats as devilled eggs, trifle, split pea soup and poached pears. Main meals were served with gravy or white sauce – or mint sauce if it was lamb – which was mopped up with a slice of bread. Breakfasts were cereal, toast, or eggs, lunch either a sandwich or cold meat and salad, and every summer Marge prepared a batch of cordial, which she made by boiling up a pound of sugar with a bottle of cordial essence.

Milk was delivered each day, left in glass bottles on the doorstep, and the baker, butcher and greengrocer all delivered as well. Meat was kept in the old Coolguardie safe, until the advent of the Coleman Cooler ice chest. This was a small box made of galvanised steel with a special tray in the top, and each day the ice man came round to top up the tray with ice. This meant that food could keep for a little longer, but there were no freezers yet so meat still had to be delivered every few days.

Because there was no way to keep food fresh for more than a day or two, women had to cook every day, and leftovers had to be eaten the next day. The only food designed to keep for a long time came in tins, and the 1950s was an inventive time for the tinned food industry. Devilled ham, beef stew, corned beef, Heinz Beans and Spaghetti, condensed milk, Hunter's Steak & Kidney Pudding, tomato soup, fruit salad and pineapple rings were just some of the many new delicacies that women could choose from at that time.

For everything else Marge had to go shopping in town, so once a week she took the bus in, pushing the baby Greg in his pram. This was no problem for the buses then, as once Marge had scooped the baby out the driver hooked up the pram to the back of the bus and off they'd go. If there was any heavier shopping that she needed she had to wait for the weekend when she and Jack could go in the car.

In the afternoons she walked back to the kindergarten to pick up Katherine, and then she spent the evenings getting them fed and bathed and helping Ron if he had homework. She always looked forward to Jack being home on weekends, and he loved it too and missed them when he was away. Sometimes in the winter months, when the weather was bad, flooding blocked the roads so he couldn't get home, but otherwise he was always home by Friday evening and he cherished the time with his family. He read to them sometimes in the evenings too, and when he was home the toddler Katherine insisted that only Jack could change her nappy, leaving Marge feeling rather disgruntled.

They didn't do much on the weekends, as they were still living on Jack's shearing wage and paying off the house and car, but Jack enjoyed spending time with the children and helped Marge with them as much as he could. They loved piggy backs, sitting up on his shoulders or being wheeled around in the wheelbarrow. He played football with the boys, and sometimes Jim, Eileen and their children visited and everyone joined in for a game of cricket. They didn't see much of Grandfather Frederick, although he did sometimes take the children for rides in his dark blue Austin A30 ute. They also had their friends Roger and Vaughan living nearby, on a fruit block in Merbein less than half an hour's drive from Mildura, and they enjoyed visiting and catching up with them while the children played games and ran around among the vines.

When he wasn't with the children, Jack spent all his spare time in his garden, tending his vegetables or pruning flowers. They didn't have a television, but of course there was the wireless, and they had an old gramophone which they used to listen to their small collection of records. The 1950s was a changing era of music, and while the influence of jazz lingered, it was mixed with – and by the end of the decade had been replaced by – blues, country and rock'n'roll. Marge liked most music, but her record collection predominantly featured her old favourites of Nat King Cole, Bing Crosby, Louis Armstrong, Frank Sinatra and Dean Martin, reminiscent of the dancing days of her youth. Of her children, her son Greg was the most taken with the gramophone, and when, at about three years old, Marge found him piling it up with ten or more records at a time, she taught him how to use it properly and he followed her instructions diligently. Any time he was home he wanted to have music on, and whenever he was sick Marge dragged his cot into the lounge and put a record on, which always seemed to soothe him.

On Sundays they went to church at St Margaret's on Eleventh Street, and sometimes in the evenings the whole family went out together to the trots. It was free for the children, making it an affordable night out, and they loved cheering on the horses with the rest of the crowd. Sometimes there was a merry-go-round, or perhaps they had an ice cream as an extra special treat.

Once a year in October they had a day out at the Mildura show, and the children loved to look at the animals, while Marge had a chance to admire the knitting and baking displays. Jack, of course, always wanted to see the vegetable and garden shows. It was a whole day out, with rides and treats, and Marge never failed to pack sandwiches and cakes for lunch. They were simple times, but they were special, and these carefree days with the whole family out having fun together became some of her most treasured and cherished memories.

In the first week of November they celebrated Guy Fawkes night, and the townspeople built up a big bonfire for the children to sit and play around. Ron and his cousin Wayne saved for months to buy crackers for the celebrations, which they mostly used to blow up their neighbours' letterboxes, but one year Marge tried combining Guy Fawkes night with Ron's birthday party, and Jack got hold of some sparklers and penny bangers for them – a kind of small firecracker. Ron and Wayne, in a fit of mischievous curiosity not unlike their fathers', thought it would be fun to find out what would happen if they lit a stack of the crackers all at once, and told Greg to hold them while they lit them and retreated. Greg nearly had his hands blown off, Jack lost his temper and raged at his son and his nephew until he ran out of steam, and that was the first and last Guy Fawkes birthday party.

At the beginning of 1954 there was some excitement in Mildura when the Queen and Prince Philip visited as part of a Royal Tour of Australia. It was a historic moment – it was the first time a reigning monarch had visited the country and the newly crowned Queen and her handsome husband brought with them the hope of peace in the post-war years. They arrived in Mildura on Thursday, March 25, where 50,000 people – quite a number considering the population at the time was only 10,000 – were waiting to greet them. Marge was there with the infant Greg and several other young mothers from the preschool, as part of the large crowd lining the street cheering and waving flags – one of the local scout groups even wore kilts for the occasion. They watched as the Queen, dressed in a floral two piece and white gloves, rode with the royal party from Henderson Park and up Deakin Avenue to a podium on the corner of 8th Street. Here the procession was greeted by the Mayor, Councillor W J Christie and his wife, and the Queen was presented with a bouquet of local roses by a local school girl, ten-year-old Joan Taylor. The local gardening committee had decorated the dais with bunches of grapes and paper leaves to represent the local grape growing industry, and despite the warm day – and feeling slightly unwell from the flight – the Queen stood and smiled to the crowd as several dignitaries made speeches and a number of prominent locals were presented to her. Marge stood watching, full of admiration for this young woman, only a year older than she was, who carried the hopes of the Commonwealth on her small but resilient shoulders. Later that day The Queen and Prince Philip visited a vineyard in Red Cliffs, a short drive out of town in the heart of Sunraysia territory, where they found another 30,000 people waiting to catch a glimpse of their new monarch. The royal couple then watched a short demonstration about the winemaking process and were presented with five tonnes of dried fruit before making their way back to Mildura to catch a flight to Perth (the dried fruit was shipped back separately to England).

It was about this time when they were living in Mildura that Marge's mother Kathleen came to live with them. All her children were married now, and she must have felt it was time for a change. Perhaps she missed the second daughter that she had seen so little of for the past couple of years. She left an active life in Horsham, where she had been working as a shearers' cook and still looking after boarders in her big house, and squeezed into the tiny house with them on Sarnia Avenue. She took a job as a companion to an old lady, cooking, cleaning and running errands for her. It kept her busy for most of the week, and she joined a Bridge club as well, so despite the fact that they were in the same house Marge saw very little of her except on weekends. She still contributed what she could to the household, and helped Marge as much as she could – her company was especially welcome on the weekends when Jack wasn't home, and she made herself very useful with the old Singer machine, making shorts and trousers for the boys using the marvellous new invention of the zipper. She joined them every week for church, of course, and the children had to take extra care when they dressed on Sunday mornings with Gar casting her attentive eye over their appearance. Freddie and his new wife Merle also came up to live in Mildura, and so for a while it was like old times with so much family around them and so much going on.

Kathleen stayed with them for a year or more, until she started developing health problems. She was a heavy smoker and had begun to suffer from memory lapses and issues with concentration, not to mention bouts of melancholy which no one could cheer her out of. Nowadays she would probably be diagnosed with early onset dementia and depression, but in the 1950s very little was understood about these conditions and there was still a lot of stigma attached to them, so that it wasn't openly talked about and there was little or no support for other family members. On the doctor's recommendations, Marge and Freddie made the difficult decision to take her to a hospital in Melbourne for treatment, and they drove her down together, leaving Merle to look after the children. As she drove away from the hospital, knowing she was leaving her mother there on her own, Marge felt it was the hardest thing she'd ever had to do.

While in hospital Kathleen was treated with electroconvulsive therapy, also known as shock therapy, which involves applying electricity to the frontal lobes of the brain in order to induce a seizure. At the time it was considered a ground-breaking treatment for all types of mental health conditions from depression to schizophrenia, and one course of therapy involved two to three sessions a week for several weeks. At the time, shock therapy was not openly discussed, though most people had heard of it, and nobody other than the doctors and practitioners who administered it really knew what it was like – but no doubt it was an uncomfortable and traumatic form of treatment, and if Marge had had any idea of what her mother would be subjected to she would never have agreed to leave her there. Kathleen stayed in hospital for the full course of treatment, and then went to live with Bonny and Eric in Horsham for a while, where she was no doubt supplied with the latest in antidepressant medication, which at the time included the new discovery of lithium as a mood stabiliser, and chlorpromazine, which is still used as an anti-psychotic today.

Meanwhile, Marge was having some health problems of her own, albeit less serious ones. She now had none of her original teeth left, after having three children – there were no calcium supplements in those days so the best solution was to simply remove the teeth when enough of them had rotted or fallen out, and replace them with a denture. Fortunately this didn't present any great difficulties for Marge, who was able to leave them in all the time except for cleaning them. She had, finally, also been to see an optometrist after years of struggling with her eyesight, and was now in possession of a pair of spectacles. This made life much easier, particularly for watching things at a distance, and meant she could sit and read a book much more easily too – not that she had much time for that. She did, however, have more help at home now, after she and Jack had decided together that he should give up shearing and find a job in Mildura. Marge was feeling the strain of having three children to look after, especially now her mother was no longer there, and Jack wanted to spend more time at home with the family. He took a job at a local dairy, working on the bottling production line, which he enjoyed though he missed working outside. Some mornings he had to be up at dawn to deliver milk to the railways and shops in the area, and sometimes Katherine, whose name he had affectionately shortened to Kaysie, went along with him. He became good friends with his employers and workmates, and although he missed the shearing he still enjoyed being part of a team and felt that he was making a valuable contribution.

It was through his colleagues at the dairy that Marge and Jack made the acquaintance of Bev Antony, a young lady of 17 who became very fond of the children and was happy to babysit. Finally, after years of never going out together, Marge and Jack could have a night out on their own, usually to the movies or perhaps a friend's place. They didn't go out for dinner, as the money didn't stretch that far, but being able to see a movie – especially as they didn't have television at home – was a good enough treat for them. In the late 1950s, the movie industry, like the music industry, was going through something of a transformation. It was moving away from the singing chorus girls and wartime romances that had been the dominating themes of the 40s, and action films with a hint of mystery or danger were all the rage. This decade saw the rise of stars like James Dean in *Rebel Without a Cause*, Cary Grant in *North by Northwest*, and Humphrey Bogart in *The African Queen*. Proving that there was always a place for a pretty blonde, Marilyn Monroe's films *Gentlemen Prefer Blondes* and *Some Like it Hot* were some of the highest billing of the decade, and audiences loved a bit of romance, especially if it took place in far off or exotic places, such as in *Roman Holiday* with Audrey Hepburn. Interest in the Hollywood musical waned slightly, but stars like Gene Kelly kept the box office ticking over with his performances in *Singin' in the Rain* and *An American in Paris*. John Wayne had brought the American Western to Australian audiences with *The Quiet Man* in 1952, and Hitchcock's *Strangers on a Train* gave everyone a new taste for thrillers.

Marge loved them all, and though the opportunity to go didn't come up very often, she relished the chance when it did. She even took Ron to the movies once, a special treat for him one weekend when Jack was home, to see *Seven Brides for Seven Brothers*.

Jack worked at the dairy for a couple of years, but he missed being out in the fresh air and in time an opportunity came up for a general labourer at a small vineyard property about twenty minutes out of town in Gol Gol, just across the border into New South Wales. The job came with accommodation for the whole family, and it seemed to Marge and Jack like a perfect opportunity for them to have a bit more space. Jack gave up the job at the dairy, the family moved into the small house on the farm, and the children were enrolled at the local school in Gol Gol.

This was different work than Jack was used to, but it was varied and he enjoyed working outside again. Once the grape picking season was finished there was pruning to be done, as well as spraying and weeding, and any other jobs that needed doing around the farm. The couple who owned the property were lovely people and became good friends, and as usual Marge was well-supplied with fresh produce. Even so, they never had any spare money, and Jack, ever on the look-out for an opportunity, was not above nominating his wife for unpleasant tasks. After proudly boasting to the farmer's wife that his own wife could 'do anything', she inquired politely as to whether or not she could sew. "Oh yes," he said proudly. "My Marge can do anything – of course she can sew!" And before Marge could say anything about it, he committed her to doing all the farmer's mending. What could she do? She hated sewing, but Jack had said she would do it, so do it she must. She was paid for it at least, so she endured it, fitting it in when the children were at school.

They passed a pleasant couple of years at the farm, but eventually began to wish for more space of their own. A block of land came up for sale on the outskirts of Mildura, and they had plans approved to build a house on it. Their savings would only cover half of it to start with, but with all that land Jack would be able to grow a surplus of vegetables which he could sell on the weekends, so it wouldn't be long before they could finish the build. Once the half-house was ready, they packed up their things once again and moved back into Mildura.

Right: Marge's parents, Kathleen and Robert Stevenson, at her sister Bonny's wedding, April 1945. This was the last time anyone in the family ever saw or heard from Robert again.

Below: Kathleen on the day of her wedding to Robert, May 1925.

Right below: Robert's military photos, taken on his enlistment in May 1940.

Above: Stevenson family photo, circa 1942. *Rear*: Shirley, Bonny, Robert, Marge. *Seated*: Norma, Kathleen, Freddie. Marge, at 15, is wearing one of Bonny's dresses to look older, much to the disapproval of her mother.

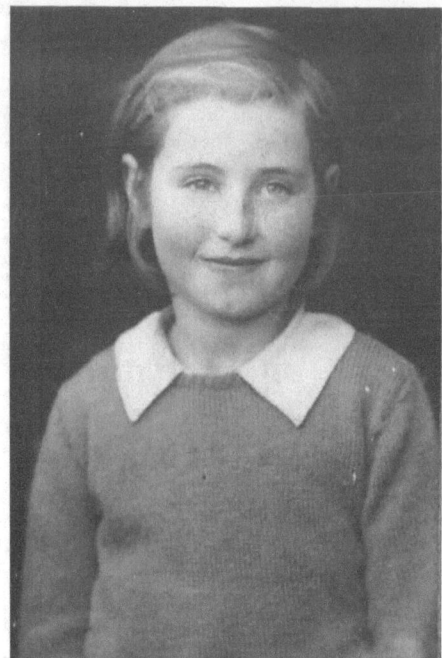

Left: Marge at 8 or 9 years old, circa 1935.

Below: Bonny, Shirley and Marge, striking a pose, Bankstown circa 1931.

Bottom: Full Bass Hill Primary School photo in 1933, with Marge seated 4th from the right, middle row.

> 4/8/41.
>
> Marjorie Stevenson was a pupil of the Bankstown Domestic Science School for eighteen (18) months. She has not attained a high scholastic standard though she is a girl of fair ability, and should have done better.
>
> I can recommend her as honest and reliable and think she would do very well at some form of manual work, for she is sensible and practical.
>
> E. M. Wheeler. (Mistress)

Above: The reference letter from Marge's school headmistress, Miss Wheeler, describing her as '*a girl of fair ability who should have done better*'.

Right: Marge, Norma, Bonny and Shirley holding their friend's baby, dressed in frocks made for them by Kathleen.

Above: Jack in his military uniform, soon after he enlisted in October 1941 at the age of 19.

Left: Frederick Stevens, with sons Jack and Jim, in Victoria in the 1920s.

Below: Jack and his mother, Katherine 'Kitty' Stevens, cicra 1922-23.

Below: The nine Stevens siblings at Ivan's wedding. *Rear*: Mable, Mary, Pat, Jean, Jess, June. *Seated*: Jack, Ivan, Jim.

Above: Marge and Bonny, ready for the dances, circa 1941.

Above: Picnicking at Green Lake in the 1940s.

Right: Jack and Marge on their honeymoon in Tasmania, 1947.

Top left: Marge and Jack on an outing in the Grampians in the early days of their courtship, 1946.
Top right: Marge on her wedding day, wearing the pearls Jack had given her as a wedding gift.
Above: Marge and Jack's bridal party, 5 April, 1947 – *from left*: Doug Bone, Mary Stevens, Ivan Stevens, Norma Stevenson, Jack, Marge, Jim Stevens, Shirley Stevenson.

Right: Marge's children, Greg, Kaysie, Ron and Chic in the garden at 11th Street, Mildura in 1957.

Above: Jack with baby Chic in Mildura and the old Fargo ute in the background.

Right: Marge with Ron going to the Horsham Show.

Right: Jack with (from left-to-right) Ron, Greg and Kaysie, with something Jack grew behind them.

Below: Jack hard at work shearing at the Gawler show, 1972.

Bottom: The family swapped their house for a caravan to live on the sheep stations of Victoria, April 1952.

Left: The Christmas Pageant in 1984 – Marge, dressed as a clown, with grandchildren Belinda, Shane and Karleen.

Below: Robert's father and Marge's grandfather, Walter Henry Stevenson, in his gladioli field.

Left: Adelaide circa 1980 – *from left:* Greg, Belinda, Shane and Ron. In jumpers knitted by Marge.

Top left: Marge and Jack on their European holiday in 1985.

Top right: Jack in his beloved Norwood Redlegs gear.

Above left: Chic and Kaysie, at Kaysie's wedding, April 1992.

Right: Jack escorts Chic through his garden on her wedding day, December 1995.

Right: On the ice in Antarctica, 2008 – surrounded by penguins.

Below: Marge, middle left, at Anzac Cove in Gallipoli, Turkey. Braving the freezing cold and crowds for the centenary of Gallipoli landings on Anzac Day, 2015.

Above: Marge and Jack with all their grandchildren on their 50th wedding anniversary, in the lounge room of their home in Arthur Steet.

Left: Marge looking out over the great Pyramids of Giza, December 2010.

CHAPTER NINE

Collective Efforts

***

The new house would be the start of a new era. It was slightly out of town, about five kilometres up the road on 11th Street, on the other side of the railway line which formed part of the boundary of the property. The half house was small, but they had plenty of space outside and at least Marge could decorate it as she liked. She had an extra sitting room, with a fireplace that kept the whole house warm, two bedrooms and a large kitchen with floor to ceiling cupboards. It had a veranda running all the way around it, a separate laundry out the back, and a big shed for Jack to keep all his work and gardening tools in.

The family-sized lounge room doubled as a dining room and they ate all their meals at the table together, unless the weather was fine or they had visitors, when they sat outside. Roger and Vaughan came to visit, and sometimes so did Freddie and Merle or Jim and Eileen. They had plenty of shade to sit under, with trees all around the property, and they had a lot of picnics and parties out in the garden. There was plenty of space for Jack and the boys to kick the football, and only once did the football end up in the middle of the afternoon tea, causing a general ruckus before Marge sent them promptly down to the bottom of the garden.

The children loved having more space, too, and there was plenty of land to explore. There was an old olive tree at the bottom of the property which gave them olives every year, and each spring Kaysie and Greg picked the wild asparagus that grew along the railway line. In summer Greg loved to wander further down the plot to catch yabbies in an old irrigation channel, which Marge then cooked up in the old copper. Ron found ways of contributing as well, and he and his friend Jimmy were frequently seen cycling off to the river with their fishing rods. They often stayed well into the evening, which inevitably led to arguments when they got home – it seemed that Ron and his mother had very different interpretations of the phrase 'be home by dark' – but Ron soon learned that if he turned up with a catch he was usually forgiven, and a dinner of fresh fish was always a welcome change from lamb.

It seemed Ron had also inherited his father's eye for opportunity, and Jimmy was usually willing to go along with him. Seeing a chance to earn a few coins, Ron was always begging his mother for a piece of spare meat, which he sometimes got, and on those days the two boys would tie it to a piece of string and dropped it over the bridge into the river to attract leeches. If the request for meat was denied they drew straws, and the loser had to roll his trousers up, wade in and wait for the leeches to attach themselves to his legs. Then they pulled them off, threw them into a bucket and cycled down to the hospital, where they sold them for a shilling apiece.

The children had to catch the bus to school now, though fortunately Ron was old enough to look after the younger ones and Snowy the Labrador had joined the family and he always walked with them to the bus stop. Every afternoon he walked back to wait for them in the same place, sitting patiently until the bus dropped them off again.

They couldn't walk to church any more, so on Sundays they had to get up early, get dressed into their best clothes and pile into Jack's old Fargo ute. Most mornings it started with no trouble, but sometimes it didn't, and it added a bit of suspense to life each Sunday morning waiting to find out which it would be. The children sat patiently in the back of the ute waiting for their father to turn the crank – if it didn't start, the children would cheer from the back of the car while Jack got angrier and sweatier, and the sniggers and whoops from the children only increased his ire. They listened to him swear and curse, turning the crank uselessly, and when he finally admitted defeat the children slipped quietly back into the house to change and disappear off into the paddocks to play. He was just as angry the time he managed to reverse over Marge's push bike which was parked at the back of the house. The children kept very quiet on that drive, fingers in mouths to keep them from laughing – but Marge didn't really mind, she hated riding the bike anyway.

Once they'd moved into the new house Jack hoped to set up an income from horticulture, so he built a large, undercover area where he planted several fruit and citrus trees. Unfortunately it took up a lot of his time – not to mention water – and any potential income was a few seasons away at least, so he had no choice but to resume his work as a shearer and was once again away for most of the week. For the first time in a couple of years Marge found herself home on her own with the children, although Ron was now old enough to take on some of Jack's responsibilities around the house. She resumed her routine of washing on Mondays and ironing on Tuesdays, collecting eggs each day, cooking for herself and the children, and catching the bus into town when she needed to. She wasn't on her own for long though, as some time after the move Kathleen returned to Mildura to live with them. She was no longer well enough to work, and although she did go out to play cards her health had now deteriorated so much that her presence was more an issue of dependency than of assistance. Some days were better than others, and although Marge did not begrudge the care her mother needed, it did add an extra worry.

Having the big property proved to be a blessing at least, as it provided them with plenty to eat. The vegetable patch was growing well and they had plenty of chickens, which they kept mainly for eggs but every so often Jack killed one for the meat. Jack also kept pigs from time to time, which meant that roughly once a year they had a glut of pork and bacon – another nice change from lamb. For a while they kept ducks as well, for the eggs, and sometimes for Christmas they bought one to eat, as it was much cheaper than buying a turkey. The downside was that they had to pluck it themselves, which Marge was quite prepared to do, but it so happened one year that on a warm afternoon before Christmas Jack and his brother Jim were relaxing on the back veranda after having enjoyed a few pre-holiday beers in the pub. They were in a very festive mood, and between them they decided it was a good time to pluck the two ducks that Marge had waiting for Christmas dinner. They set to their work in high spirits and obviously didn't notice that the back door was open, and it was Kathleen who got home first and found them still at work on the back veranda and feathers floating all through the house. She banished them both so that she could finish the job properly, and they left in the same high spirits, congratulating each other on having come up with such a jolly endeavour. Alas, it wasn't quite so amusing for Marge, who was still finding feathers in the house several days later.

1956 arrived and there were more exciting times to come, starting with an environmental emergency which involved the entire population of Mildura. A concurrence of several unlikely weather events, including higher-than-average rainfall in western Queensland, caused the Murray and Darling rivers to burst their banks, resulting in floods all the way from Wentworth in New South Wales to Mannum in South Australia – a distance of some 300 kilometres. In some places the water rose by three or four metres and spread a hundred kilometres from its original course, leaving several towns, roads and farms underwater.

Mildura, situated right in the middle of the Murray-Darling Basin area and very close to where the two rivers meet, was right in the flood path. The townsfolk rose gloriously to the occasion, led mostly by returned soldiers and farmers who used their tractors and trailers to fill sandbags with dirt, tree stumps and whatever they could find. Levies were built along the main roads and around important buildings and sirens were set up at the town hall and post office to signal when help was required. The Mildura migrant camp was re-designated as a shelter for the 200 people whose homes were flooded and they were well fed with pies delivered by the Salvation Army and a donation of rum from the Red Cliffs Club. Farmers who still had fruit and vegetables to sell delivered them by boat or flying fox.

Fortunately Marge and the children were not in danger, situated as they were at a higher elevation outside the town, but Jack had been away shearing at the time and could not get back to them for several weeks. Marge had also discovered she was pregnant again, and so she became even more wary of venturing too far from the house, although she and the children were curious enough to wander along the river sometimes to see where the water was up to. Back in Sarnia Avenue, the water had come right up to the pavement but thankfully not into anyone's homes, which Jim and Eileen, who had a new baby, Robyn, were particularly grateful for.

The floods reached their peak in August when the rest of the country was preoccupied with the upcoming Melbourne Olympics – due to be opened by Prince Philip – and so very little outside help was forthcoming. In some places the water was rising by two centimetres every hour, and local authorities began to fear for the Mildura and Red Cliffs power stations – since they not only provided power to the town but were also responsible for pumping out the town's sewerage, engineers were naturally keen to protect them from flooding and overflowing. Efforts were redoubled to bank the areas around the stations, and thankfully they were spared, though dozens of the region's vineyards and citrus farms were not so lucky.

It was several months before the waters fully receded. Thanks to the collective efforts of the townspeople and the emergency services, no lives were lost, although the local fruit industry was devastated. Scientists called it a once-in-a-hundred-year flood, and authorities declared it the biggest peace-time mobilization in the country's history. For the locals, it was just a case of getting on and doing what they could.

Things settled down and Jack returned to the family, but as ever change was never far away. In October of that year, after spending two weeks in the Mildura hospital, Jack's father Frederick passed away, and shortly after that Jim and Eileen moved with their three children from Mildura to South Australia. Things were quiet until the beginning of 1957 when the family gained a new addition – another daughter, Christine Marie, born on January 3. From now on, all of Marge's time would be taken up with caring for the baby and the others. At least pre-packaged baby food was now available, which saved one job, and Greg was big enough to toddle alongside the pram, which was now occupied by his baby sister.

They were a large, happy family, but by now things were becoming distinctly cramped with seven of them all squeezed into half a house – Kathleen was sharing one of the bedrooms with the three older children, and the baby Christine was in a cot in Marge and Jack's room. There was no room for house guests, although they made an exception for Marge's grandfather Walter – Robert's father – who came to visit only once, forcing the boys onto the lounge for a few nights until he returned to Maryborough.

This arrangement carried on until February of 1958, when Walter passed away and left them a modest sum of money. They used it to convert the veranda into rooms for the boys and for Kathleen, so Marge and Jack took the larger, now vacant bedroom, and Kaysie moved into the small one with Christine.

This new arrangement improved things considerably, and Jack must have been in a good mood one day when he decided, since they had plenty of space, to buy a cow. It would live in a field behind the property, and Jack, assuring Marge that she wouldn't have to milk it, undertook to do so twice a day. For a while they enjoyed having their own fresh milk and letting it separate to get the cream, and Ron and his friend Jimmy discovered a new source of revenue in the form of the worms that lived under the fresh cow pats, which they could sell for a shilling for fifty. Unfortunately, the cow was a lively beast and milking often left Jack with a nasty bruise or two. One day, things went a little bit too far for Jack to tolerate when the end of the rope that should have been tied to the fence came free and the cow took off. Chasing the cow would have been bad enough, but by a stroke of bad luck the loop somehow got tangled around Jack's leg and he was dragged off behind the cow, who made a good couple of laps around the field before Jack could free himself. Fortunately, he wasn't seriously injured, but his fury with the animal was something to behold and his children reported learning a few new words that day. He didn't have the means to shoot the cow then and there, as he expressed desire to do, so she was left loose in the field while Marge tended Jack's cuts and bruises. There was no cure for Jack's pride, however, and so the unfortunate cow went to the market the following Monday.

By 1960 it was becoming apparent that Kathleen's health was deteriorating more rapidly, and the earlier hardships of her life were catching up with her. She had never discovered what had happened to Robert, and her efforts to divorce him in 1950 had come to nothing as no one had been able or willing to disclose his whereabouts. It had now been fifteen years since she had seen or heard from him, and the stress of having to work constantly to support her family had turned her into a much harder and more bitter woman than the one who had been so happy to look after her grandchildren in Horsham. She spent more and more time in her room, smoking in the bed and only emerging to meet her bridge group and attend church. She had little time for her grandchildren now and couldn't stand their noise, and they learnt to tiptoe around the house so she wouldn't start scolding them. Meanwhile, Marge became more and more worried.

Kathleen's memory lapses became more frequent too, and Marge could tell that she was unhappy, but there wasn't much she could do for her other than to make sure that her physical needs, at least, were met. Doctors had prescribed her chloral hydrate and barbiturate, both of which were in common use at the time as sedatives and for combatting insomnia, and Marge kept them locked away in a high cupboard in the kitchen where she could administer them according to the doctors' instructions.

There came a time, towards the end of 1960, when Kathleen must have decided that she didn't want to cope any more, or that she would no longer be a burden, or perhaps both. It may be that she knew her health was failing, and didn't want to hang around for it to get worse. Either way, one night in early November she found a way to get into the medicine cabinet when no one was around and took all her medicines back to her room. The next morning, the 3rd, when Marge noticed she was late getting up, she sent Greg in to wake her for breakfast, and so it was her grandson who was the first to try and fail to wake her. He called out to his mother who followed him in to the bedroom and found her mother lying lifeless in the bed with her empty medicine bottles beside her. Kathleen was 55 years old, and Marge was only 33.

It was a sharp and tragic blow. Jack was away shearing so Marge was on her own, but thankfully she was on good terms with the neighbours and they were a huge support to her now. The children were sent to stay with them while the police and coroner were called, and her friend Pat Davis came to stay with her until Jack returned from work. She handled it all in the best way she could, overwhelmed as she was with shock and sadness. Her doctor was a great support, and Freddie and Bonny came up to help her with arrangements and to stay for the funeral.

Kathleen was buried in Mildura in the grounds of St Margaret's, the church she had attended every Sunday for the past few years. December followed, and it was a much quieter Christmas that year without Kathleen's famous roast dinner and Christmas pudding. In the new year an inquest was held, and on January 11 the coroner ruled her death as suicide by overdose, confirming what the family already knew, or at least suspected. Kathleen had made her choice, and now they had to move on.

It was a hard time for Marge. She felt the loss of her mother keenly, and Jack's efforts to sell vegetables hadn't been as successful as they'd hoped, so despite their best intentions they had been unable to finish building the house. In their usual spirit, they rolled up their sleeves and got on with things, but inevitably, more change was on the way. Jack received a message from his brother Jim, asking him to go into business with him once again, this time buying, shearing and selling sheep. It didn't take them long to decide – they had no family left in Mildura now and Jack had loved running a business with his brother in Horsham – so once again they made the decision to pack up the family and move, this time to a small town called Sandy Creek, just outside the city of Adelaide in South Australia.

CHAPTER TEN

Red and Blue Blooded

***

They applied for a trust home in Gawler, and in the meantime they moved into a farmhouse with Jim and Eileen on the road between Gawler and Lyndoch. Things were quite crowded, but it was only temporary and the children, especially, loved being with their cousins again. They had two new ones now, Sharon and Louis, bringing the number of residents up to 13. Unfortunately Snowy the Labrador didn't come with them – he'd been given to one of Jack's shearing friends before they left Mildura.

Jim and Jack spent the days working, so Marge and Eileen had a much quieter house to enjoy during the week. Each day the older children rode their bikes to the local school at Sandy Creek and back, and when they weren't at school they spent most of their time outside, playing in the empty tennis court or exploring the big paddock out the back. The property sat on a particularly sharp bend in the road, and on some mornings they went outside to find an overturned car leaning against the trees on the other side, which they always found very fascinating.

Meanwhile, Jack and Jim were still coming up with plans that weren't very successful, but at least kept the children amused. For example, the big paddock had a row of very large, very old red gum stumps. They decided, for reasons best known to themselves, to remove them, and it took two or three days and several tins of petrol to finally get them burning. As soon as they did, one of the neighbours appeared, screeching round the bend in his van and running across the paddock with his arms waving manically, to point out there was a total fire ban in place and they had better put them out. That took another day to do, and they were lucky to escape the attention of the authorities.

They stayed with Jim and Eileen for eight or nine months before a house in Evanston became available for them, and the family had its own home once again. Christine started school in 1962 (although by now she had acquired the nickname 'Chic', which Des had unwittingly given her by singing 'Chicory Chic' whenever he visited), and so for the first time since she was married Marge found herself at home by herself during the day. Not that she had any free time – the new house didn't have many modern conveniences, and Marge had to make do with a lot of old fashioned – and therefore more time consuming – methods. For heating water she had an old chip heater, which was a cylindrical, metal unit with a fire box and flue. To heat the water, she had to light a fire in the bottom of the unit – using wood chips, newspaper or whatever was around – and the water was circulated through the flue to heat up. It worked, but it was slow and also dangerous, as the water was connected directly to the shower and if the fire was too hot then the water would be scalding. At least Marge's cooking was much improved from the days of her youth when she avoided it by polishing furniture – her Sunday roasts were now a treat that everyone looked forward to, and Jack of course kept her well supplied with home grown vegetables.

Unfortunately, the new house wasn't connected to the sewerage – instead they had a septic tank in the bottom of the garden which often overflowed, so they had to open it up to drain it out onto the paddock behind them. There was no escaping its pungent effects on those days, and the next-door neighbour was always ready to share her views on the subject. It wasn't very pleasant for the residents either, but there was nothing they could do about it, and in any case Jack said it was good for the vegetables. Its main problem was that it wasn't fenced off, so it was only a matter of time before someone fell in. Alas, it was Kaysie who went out one evening to pick some corn, not realising that the tank was open. She was freshly bathed and in a clean dressing gown when she lost her footing and in she went with a repugnant splash. The others heard her scream and ran outside to find her clambering back out again, covered in sewage from head to foot. She was sent promptly back into the shower while her siblings pinched their noses and tried not to laugh.

Meanwhile, the farming venture that had brought the family down to Adelaide was not going very well. The premise was a reasonable one – Jim would buy the sheep, Jack would shear them, Jack's friend Des – an old friend from his days on the road – would class the wool, and then the sheep and wool would all be sold on again. But they were not farmers – patience was not a virtue either of them possessed in any great amount – and the strain took its toll. In the end they gave up on the business and Jack went back to shearing in and around Gawler. Fortunately, the work was mostly local so Jack didn't have to stay away very often, and Marge had his help and his company most evenings and weekends, which she was very happy about.

Jack loved being home as well. He was, above all other things, a family man, and he loved his wife and his children. His greatest pleasure (along with gardening, of course) was spending time with them, and now that Ron was in high school he was bringing home work which was beyond the scope of Marge's limited schooling. Jack, on the other hand, was a dab hand with numbers, and could help him easily. Ron, in turn, helped the others.

In time the boys both joined the local scouting club, and Jack took them along to meetings in the evenings. Eventually – possibly to save the extra trip – he decided to join as well, and on March 27, 1962 he was appointed Assistant Scout Master, and then on July 24 he was appointed as a Scouter, which made him one of the club leaders. He followed the boys' football as well and was always there to watch their games on the weekends. At the same time, the girls were getting into dancing. They both joined the local calisthenics club, and Marge added making costumes and sewing sequins to her long list of duties. She loved to watch them dance though, and was always there at competitions, or making snacks for the many friends Kaysie invited round to practice dancing in the garden.

As usual, life was busy and fulfilling and they had no trouble settling into a new town. Sometimes friends or family came to stay, and they squeezed into the small house and everyone enjoyed the extra company for a while. They joined the local Anglican community at the Church of the Transfiguration in Gawler South, Marge joined a mother's group, and in her usual way made plenty of friends in her new town. Sometimes she needed to go into Gawler, and although she had a bike, she didn't really like riding it and preferred to make the one hour walk each way. She wasn't interested in learning to drive – Jack had tried to teach her once but inevitably they'd argued through the whole thing, so that was the first and last driving lesson. Sometimes she took the train, if she had things to carry, and when Ron learned to drive he gave her a lift sometimes too. There was always a way, and as was her habit she looked for solutions and usually found them.

The 60s swung along and life was good, though the global situation caused some concern. The War in Vietnam was showing no signs of slowing down, and in 1964 the Australian government introduced a selective conscription scheme, which they called National Service, to assist the

American allied forces. Each year a contingent of twenty-year-old men was selected by ballot, and they were chosen by way of a barrel with wooden marbles, each numbered between 1 and 365. Those whose birthdays fell on the days that were drawn were required to present themselves for two years full-time national service, to be followed by three and a half years part-time. In 1968 – the year Ron turned twenty – the family waited nervously for the ballot results, but fortunately Ron's birthdate was not selected. Had he been born a day later, on the third of November, he would have had to go. The scheme ended in 1972, and the Americans withdrew from Vietnam early in 1973, so when Greg turned 20 later that year there was thankfully no ballot to worry about. The children grew up and Ron left school to attend technical college. His early inclination to tinker with machines (and door hinges) was now his passion and he hoped to take up an apprenticeship at Holden's. Greg loved to play music and dreamed of travelling the world, and the girls were always dancing. The house was feeling smaller and smaller and finally they decided it was time to buy a bigger one of their own.

Becoming homeowners once again was not an easy road. In the late 1960s the average price of a new home was around $10,000, but the average weekly wage was only around $60, so while Jack's shearing was providing for their daily needs, saving for a deposit and mortgage would take considerably more funds. They talked about it together, and decided it was time for Marge to return to the workforce. With the children being older and more independent, and new appliances which meant she didn't have to spend whole days washing, ironing and cooking, she had more free time than ever, and Marge, who liked to be busy and wanted to contribute, was willing to give it a go.

Through a friend at church they discovered an opening at John Martin's – a big department store in the nearby town of Elizabeth – so she applied and got the job. It was a scary and daunting prospect for Marge, who was now approaching 40 years old and had been out of the workforce for nearly two decades. She found herself working with a lot of young, unmarried women – much like she had been when she had worked at GJ Coles – and she found that a lot of things had changed in the meantime. To start with, the currency had changed, and now she was dealing with dollars and cents instead of pounds, shillings and pence, and the recent invention of the credit card meant she had to process a paper slip and collect a signature with each transaction. Not surprisingly, she jumped straight in despite her fears, and with encouragement from Jack and the children she set about learning everything she could.

She worked on the sales floor with three or four other ladies and each one of them was allocated a section of the store. She was placed in the menswear section and her job was to arrange the clothes, keep everything tidy, assist customers and sometimes work the till. Fortunately it didn't take long for all her old skills to come back to her – she loved talking to people and was still good at handling money. Her manager was an interesting character who was often disappearing into the office to take a nip from his hipflask, but he wouldn't tolerate any idleness in his staff, even if there were no customers – so Marge spent a lot of time folding and refolding clothes. Despite his idiosyncrasies, he was a fair man who recognised good work, and every Christmas he insisted that the ladies each have an hour off so they could do their Christmas shopping.

Marge started off part-time and most days she worked from 10 in the morning till 4 in the afternoon, so after sending the children and Jack off to school and work she walked to the train station for the short ride into Elizabeth. Once Greg was old enough to buy a motorbike he sometimes gave her a lift in, and then she caught the train back home again. Ron was usually home from work before she was, so he kept an eye on the others until Marge was home, usually by about 4:30, when she would get dinner for everyone. As Christmas and other celebrations approached she found herself with more and more shifts so she was almost working full time, and well into the evenings on Fridays. This was thanks to a loophole in the Early Closing Act which required shops in the Metropolitan area to close at 5.30 p.m. on weekdays. As Elizabeth was classed as a developing area it was not included in the Act, so shops stayed open until 9 p.m. – a benefit which shoppers and retailers took full advantage of.

Late night shopping shifts were extremely busy times and Marge found she could hardly move in the store for the crowds of people crammed in. She still enjoyed it though, and her manager showed his faith in her by placing her on the till, which she handled much better than many of her younger colleagues. Jack also made the most of the later opening hours and came in with the car, so he could do his own shopping and to give Marge a lift home when she finished. Elizabeth was finally included in the Act in 1970, but until then it was the place to go for late night shopping.

Marge loved being back at work. It was a welcome change from the routine of looking after the family, and she enjoyed the camaraderie of being part of a team. Jack's shearing work brought in enough to see them through each week, and Marge's wages went into the mortgage fund. Anything they didn't need, they saved. Jack grew his vegetables as usual, and of course there was always a steady supply of lamb. The children still had their dancing, football and scouts, but Marge and Jack did very little themselves. They spent their evenings and weekends at home or visiting friends – there were no trips to restaurants or cinemas, and no holidays unless they could stay with family. Eventually they found a home, only a couple of kilometres away in Evanston Park, and after digging up every coin they could find, in every money box, under every cushion and down the back of every chair, they put down their deposit and were home owners once more.

At last they had more space, and the children could spread out and invite their friends over. There were still only three bedrooms so they had to share, but they had more living space and a bigger garden with a large, empty paddock just behind it, perfect for kicking footballs. Jack set up a new veggie garden, of course, and since he had space he planted some fruit trees as well. Marge was able to finally organise a new kitchen – there was no chip heater anymore, as the 60s saw the introduction into most households of the gas water boiler, but one of the greatest luxuries of the new house was an electric fridge, which meant Marge could store food for longer, and therefore go shopping less often, and she could save leftovers for another day or even two. She also had a new gas cooker, although it took a bit of getting used to. There was at least one scary incident when, after turning the gas on to prepare the dinner, she was distracted by the children coming home from school and asking questions. When she finally struck the match there was a great boom – fortunately she escaped with just some singed eyebrows.

Life for the Australian housewife changed dramatically in the 60s. Household appliances were becoming more affordable and electricity was the new way to do things. This decade alone saw the invention of the electric vacuum cleaner (the most popular being the upright Dynamatic), electric food mixers (every woman who aspired to win a baking contest wanted a Sunbeam Mixmaster) and electric percolators. Many homes now had their own telephones, and those with the budget could get their hands on electric hairdryers, electric toothbrushes and electric blankets.

Later in the decade the first microwaves were introduced, but for Marge it was all about the electric washing machine. Being able to put the washing in, turn a few knobs and then pull it out ready for the clothes line, was a luxury she had spent many Mondays dreaming about. Jack was as proud as punch, therefore, when he turned up one day with a brand new, shiny twin tub electric washing machine. Much to his dismay, Marge took one look at it and made him take it back – she was not interested in a twin tub! It was promptly replaced with a single tub, top loading machine, and everyone was happy. Now that Marge didn't have to spend a whole day each week scrubbing, wringing and hanging, she had much more time for herself, and her back thanked her as well.

There came a time, also in the 60s, when Marge and Jack finally succumbed to the lure of a television. Everything was in black and white then, and by the end of the decade there were still only three stations, but it was nevertheless an enormous novelty to see moving pictures at home instead of having to go to the cinema. Most of the programming involved news, current affairs and talk shows, but variety shows and concerts were also popular and Dame Edna Everage (alter ego of Barry Humphries) became a familiar face. To begin with, television stations only broadcast for a few hours each day, but it wasn't long before it was eclipsing the radio as the nation's favourite entertainment. The 60s saw the debuts of series such as *Homicide*, *Four Corners* and the rural soap opera *Bellbird*. Children's television also had some great successes in the 60s with shows like *Play School* and *Here's Humphrey* – both of which would run for several decades – and *Skippy the Bush Kangaroo*, which enjoyed great popularity overseas.

Live satellite transmissions became possible, and the first live sporting event was the New South Wales Rugby Football League Grand Final in 1967. Other events followed, and families could watch big events like The Ashes, Wimbledon and even the Olympic games from inside their living rooms. But probably the greatest live telecasting event of the 60s was the moon landing in July of 1969, which broke the record for the longest live telecast at 163 hours and was replayed for several days afterwards. It happened in the middle of the day in Australia, and housewives at home and children at school were all glued to their television sets for the entire 2.5 hours of the landing, watching Neil Armstrong take his 'giant leap for mankind' and knowing that the rest of the world was watching with them. At the time it was the largest ever TV audience, estimated at around 600 million people. Marge and her colleagues had to watch it at work, since their manager refused to let them go home, despite the fact there was not a single customer in the store. They watched it together on the televisions in the home appliance department, full of excitement to be witnessing one of mankind's greatest collective achievements.

Colour television would not be introduced until 1975, but the nation was hooked on the television medium long before then. It was certainly popular with the Stevens family, and although they didn't have much time for it during the week they enjoyed sitting around it together on the weekends, enjoying the sports and concerts and getting to know the first generation of famous television faces. Anyone who was home on Saturday night had to sit through Jack's favourite, *Reg Lindsay's Country and Western Hour*, in which the host – Reg – led groups of square dancers around his large barn, artistically set with hay bales, bits of fences and various riding and country paraphernalia. Kaysie and Chic usually took this opportunity to practise their own dancing, at which Greg would complain loudly, adding to the general hubbub, and Ron, oblivious to all of them, sat on the floor with an old towel happily dismantling bits of cars and putting them back together again. Much more satisfactory was *The Wonderful World of Disney* on Sundays, hosted by Walt Disney himself until his death in 1966. His own rendition of his theme song, *When You Wish Upon a Star*, was an enduring feature of many happy Sunday evenings.

They had many friends in Evanston by this time. Jim and Eileen had moved to Victoria when the business didn't work out, but Jack's sister Mary (Marge's third bridesmaid) and her husband John were now living up in the Adelaide Hills with their children, and they visited each other when they could. Jack had relinquished his Scout leadership position but had become more involved with the church and was appointed Lay Reader in April 1972. The children were getting on well in school, and mostly getting on with each other. Kaysie and Greg argued the most, usually about Greg's loud music, and Chic was often being reprimanded for sneaking off to visit her boyfriend. Greg caused a great commotion once when he crashed Jack's car and ran off to hide at a friend's place for a couple of days. In each case, it was Marge's job to hand out punishments, although Jack didn't hold back from venting his spleen if he happened to be at the scene of any transgressions. But mostly, they all got on, and the children always knew they had a supporting and loving family to come home to.

The 60s became the 70s. Ron got his apprenticeship at Holden's, where he stayed, and not very long afterwards he met a young lady, Denise, at the Willaston Football Club Cabaret. Marge and Jack were delighted to see their eldest son so happy, and even more thrilled when they announced their engagement. They were married on April 17, 1971, and the day went smoothly despite thunderstorms and a flyover which prevented the congregation from hearing the wedding vows. It was an emotional day, and Jack was not ashamed to shed a few tears of happiness. Several members of their very large extended families came over to Adelaide for the celebration, and Marge and Jack had a wonderful day catching up with them all and of course gracing the dance floor in the evening.

Life carried on and the other children grew up – Kaysie earned a scholarship to attend teacher's college, and she and Chic both got part-time jobs at John Martin's. Greg spent his holidays working with Jack as a roustabout on the sheep farms, then left school in year 11 to go to Perth. That venture didn't work out, so he returned and finished year 11 before going to work at Holden's with Ron.

Ron stayed at Holden's until an opportunity came up to study at the General Motors Oshawa plant in Ontario, so he and Denise moved to Canada for a while. By this time Marge and Jack had a telephone in the house, and it was via this new medium, on December 4, 1973, that they learned of the birth of their first grandchild, Belinda. They were overjoyed at the news, though naturally Marge found it difficult being so far away. When a photo arrived in the post a couple of weeks later, she took it to work with her and showed it proudly to everyone she could find until her supervisor politely suggested she put it up on the noticeboard to save time. Despite her tender age of 46 it was clear she was excited to be a grandmother, although she would have to wait a little while before she could meet her granddaughter.

Marge and Jack carried on working and eventually they were able to pay off the house. Now they could enjoy more of a social life, and with so many friends there were always parties and birthdays to attend. They still loved a ball, and once a year they drove up to the Barossa with their friends Pete and Lee who lived around the corner, for an annual festival which included dinner and a dance. The men always enjoyed several bottles of Barossa Pearl, which was a fruity, sparkling wine based on a German Perlwein. The bottle was round at the bottom with a long, slender neck, like a Perrier bottle, and its producers had hoped it would be popular with young people. In fact, its low-alcohol content and affordability made it popular with everyone, and even Marge, who had never been a drinker, enjoyed a glass or two. The men always drove home after the dance, still quite drunk and in a manner that would alarm us today, but which they got away with then thanks to sparser traffic and less vigilant law enforcers.

Having more free time inspired Jack to try some new hobbies, and he decided one summer to attempt to make his own ginger beer. This involved making a ginger syrup, sealing it in a bottle with yeast, lemon juice and water, and leaving it in a pantry or another cool, dark place to ferment. It only needed a couple of days and then it had to be moved to the fridge, otherwise it would keep fermenting until there was too much pressure in the bottle. Inevitably, Jack left it all in the pantry for too long and it exploded, sending glass, ginger beer and the other contents of the pantry everywhere. His reaction was predictable – he shouted and swore a lot – but once he'd calmed down there was nothing for it but to clean it up and chuck it all out, leaving his children shaking their heads and wondering why he insisted on getting involved with these things.

Jack was, at his heart, a softie and a peace lover, but certain things did get him fired up and when his emotions were raised he never tried to hide or conceal them – he wore them out on his sleeve for everyone to see, and when his temper was up the children learned to stay out of his way. Any damage to or tampering with the garden was a sure way to provoke a reaction, and one of the neighbour's children had the hose turned on him a few times when he wandered absentmindedly into Jack's flowerbeds. The car was another frequent instigator of an inflamed outburst, and his complete lack of any mechanical skill or instinct didn't help matters. Nor did his tendency to act on his impulses instead of thinking them through, and his children were often left shaking their heads at his attempts to tinker with it, especially Ron, who had clearly inherited his talent for engineering from his grandfather Robert, and not his father. Shortly after jack had replaced the old Fargo ute with a blue Torana, Greg came home to find that his father had shut the keys in the boot of the car, and it now had a big hole in the back of it where he'd prised it open with a crowbar.

"Is the front of the car locked?" Greg asked him.

"No."

"Why didn't you take the partial shelf off the back and reach through to get the keys?"

Jack paused for a moment and then said, "Oh. I never thought of that."

His wife and children knew by now that Jack was best left alone in these moments until he could blow off steam and his thermostat returned to normal. But there was one thing that got him more worked up, and had a longer lasting effect than any other, and that was football.

It was shortly after they made the move to Evanston that they made the acquaintance of Kingsley Arthur 'Bill' Wedding, who was a star ruckman at the Norwood Football Club, a prominent team in the South Australian league. Norwood was nowhere near where they lived – at least a 40-minute drive towards the city – but there were no league teams local to Gawler then, and Bill was a friend, so they signed up as Norwood supporters. It was the beginning of a life-long passion, and Jack followed the fortunes of the Redlegs with his usual gusto. He went to watch them play as often as he could, sometimes at their home ground on The Parade and sometimes even further away at Football Park in West Lakes, dressed up in the club colours of red and navy blue. His enthusiasm was infectious, so that the rest of the family got caught up in his red-and-blue fever, and most weekends in winter would see them at one stadium or another, huddled up in freshly knitted red and blue scarves and beanies, and a bottle of Stone's ginger wine to keep them warm.

With the children growing up and everyone having their separate interests and activities, the football was one thing that brought them all together. There were several ups and down – the club, after several premierships in the 50s, was going through a bit of a drought in the 60s, but at least Bill was doing well: he claimed the club's best and fairest award every year between '61 and '65 and played several State of Origin games for South Australia. When a new Central District's Football Club, based in Elizabeth, joined the league in 1964, many of the locals jumped at the chance to support a club closer to home, but not the Stevenses – they were

Norwood supporters, red and blue blooded, and that was that. It was a while before their loyalty was finally rewarded, but it was worth the wait when the club took the premierships in '75 and '78.

It didn't take long for the family to learn that Jack's mood often depended on the success or failure of the Redlegs, and unfortunately his ability to get over a bad mood quickly – a defining characteristic of his entire life – seemed to desert him in the face of a Norwood defeat. He got over-excited when they won, became sullen when they lost, and always had plenty to say about the game and the umpires. He was careful never to swear in front of Marge or the girls, but he was far less restrained when it came to telling opposition supporters what he thought of them. He was never shy about sharing his opinion of their team (which was never complimentary), but if there was one thing he couldn't stand more than any other it was supporters who abused their own players – something which he resolutely refused to do, no matter how badly they played. He couldn't tolerate other fans doing it either, and even a pair of old ladies who'd come to support the opposition weren't spared his wrath when he heard them insulting their own team.

"Why did you come then, you're wasting your money if you're going to be like that', he would rage at them. Marge, while she admired the sentiment, wished he could be more circumspect, but it was a useless wish – Jack couldn't hide how he was feeling any more than he could drive them all to the moon.

It made him a target as well, and there were several times when Marge worried that he would get into a fight and his children had to restrain him. This was particularly difficult at Footy Park, where all the supporters were mixed in together on the old dirt mounds, and opposition supporters tried everything from pointed remarks about his age to throwing bits of food at Kaysie in an attempt to get a reaction from him. It often worked, and Marge spent many anxious afternoons wondering if she'd be tending a broken nose or black eye.

This was in the days before the AFL and the state league was by far the most popular sport in Adelaide. All the family enjoyed going, except Chic who preferred her dancing. Marge's work meant she couldn't always go, and sometimes she refused to because Jack's behaviour was too embarrassing, and on those occasions Jack and the children always stood up on the hill at The Parade waving red and blue flags with the other supporters. When Marge came with them they took seats in the stands, which meant that Marge spent her Monday mornings sitting on the phone, waiting to get tickets.

Sometimes they went out for dinner after the match, which was a jovial occasion following a victory, but a sombre one if they had lost. Jack sat and sulked, refused to participate in conversation and snapped at the slightest provocation. He also caused embarrassment at family occasions, including the time when they turned up at a birthday party at the home of Marge's friend Joyce, who had decorated the place in black and white, not realising they were the colours of Norwood's great rival Port Adelaide. On that occasion Jack simply grumbled until they could escape and go home, but it was all too much for him when they went to a party at Glenelg, at the home of Jack's niece Sue and her husband Barry, after having just lost to that very team. He simply couldn't keep his feelings bottled up, and denounced them very loudly to the whole room, in considerably unsavoury language. Red-faced Marge could only wish for the floor to open and swallow her up but alas, they had to wait the awkward moment out. At least Jack felt much better after his outburst, having vented his feelings at last.

And so the Norwood Football Club became part of the fabric of life. Sometimes they went for dinner dances at the club, and when grandchildren started coming along they went to the games too, and learned to kick a football on the ground during the breaks. The girls kept dancing, and Ron's career at Holden's was going well. Kaysie got teaching positions in Magill and then down in Mt Gambier, and Greg did a bit of travelling with his best mate Steve. Chic finished year 11 and then followed Kaysie to teacher's college where she studied for her primary teaching diploma, and Marge stayed content with her job at John Martin's.

With work, football and families to visit, life was never dull and Marge had plenty to keep her busy, despite no longer having to cook and clean for four children. She was on her own more often now, and she and Jack both began to feel that it was time for Jack to give up shearing. He didn't enjoy it as much any more, and he wanted to spend more time at home. They made some enquiries, and heard from their niece Sue (host of the infamous dinner party in Glenelg) that the small continental deli she worked at in the eastern suburbs of Adelaide was up for sale. Running a deli would be a complete change of lifestyle for them, but they felt ready for the challenge – and Jack, especially, was tempted at the prospect of living so close to his beloved Norwood Football Club. They put their house on the market, leaving Greg to look after it until it sold, and moved their lives into the city.

CHAPTER ELEVEN

The Continental Effect

***

It was around September 1974, when Marge was 47 and Jack 52, when they bought the Continental Deli in Burnside and moved to the eastern suburbs of Adelaide. They stayed with Mary and John for a little while, until they found a small house in Young Street about a kilometre away from the shop. It was an exciting time – neither of them had taken on a challenge like this before – but with Marge's experience in retail and Jack's in business they were confident they could give it a go. The business itself was already set up with suppliers, equipment and regular customers, and it was in a good position on a roundabout junction between two major roads – Glynburn and Greenhill – and right next to the Feathers Hotel. It was coming up to Christmas, so they only had a couple of months to settle in before things got really busy.

It didn't take them long to realise they had got a little bit more than they bargained for. The man who sold them the deli turned out have been less than honest about the state of the premises, and they found many of his goods and stocks were stale or out of date, and several of the fridge and storage units were faulty and had to be replaced. They had to spend some money doing the place up, but once that was finished they were pleased with the result. Now they were open for business, and had a few weeks to learn the ropes before the Christmas rush.

It was a good thing that both of them were accustomed to long days and working hard. It took about fifteen minutes to walk to work from where they lived, and each morning Jack was up and at the deli by 7 a.m. to receive deliveries and get the shop ready for opening at 8. Marge joined him then, and they started the day serving breakfasts and coffees to local tradespeople, and truck drivers who came through on their way towards the nearby Eastern Freeway. The Burnside Police Station was just across the road, with the council depot just behind it, so at lunch time they did a good trade in pies, pasties and sandwiches. Then they had customers who came for their continental selection, buying up cheeses, meats and cakes for their parties on the weekends. This was a specialised market that hadn't been picked up by supermarkets then, so trade was decent.

On weekdays Marge usually went home around 5 or 6 o'clock, to get dinner ready and take care of any housework. Jack stayed on until they closed at 8, then he had to tidy up and restock the fridges before heading home to do the accounts. He usually ate dinner at around 9 p.m., before collapsing into bed to recharge for the next day. This went on until Friday morning when he went in an hour earlier at 6 to clean out the meat counter and restock it, ready for the busiest day of the week. Weekends were slightly better as they closed earlier, but it was still a gruelling schedule and in those early days they had no choice but to work seven days a week.

Despite the hard work they were filled with enthusiasm, and the novelty of running their own shop and living in a city gave them the energy to keep going. Jack relished the challenge, and perhaps felt this was the chance that he couldn't take when he was young, when circumstances forced him – more than once – into the shearing trade. He loved building rapport with the customers and was very good at negotiating and upselling, and everything he'd learned at the wool shop all those years ago came back to him. Even once the excitement had worn off, and the sheer number of hours they had to put in was wearing them down, they fought off thoughts of giving up. Jack, in particular, was determined to stick it out and Marge was happy to keep going as long as Jack was.

There were plus sides to working in a deli. For one thing, they were always together, and they made a good team. Marge, with her experience working a busy counter, was responsible for keeping the place clean and tidy during the day, making lunches, serving customers at the till and generally keeping things running smoothly. As well as serving customers, Jack did all the meat slicing and weighing and all the heavy lifting of crates and bottles from the storeroom to the counters. When it came to the business side of things, Marge left it all to Jack, who had always been good with figures and could finally put his talent to good use. He took care of all the accounting, including billing and invoicing, as well as stocktaking, orders and banking. They also got to sample many of their goods, since they had to – as Marge put it – be able to tell the customers what they tasted like. She particularly liked sampling all the meats – Italian hams and salamis, Spanish chorizo and all manner of cured sausage, so different to the roasting and stewing meats she'd cooked and eaten all her life. She wasn't so excited by the cheeses, being only used to simple cheddar flavours, but they stocked a colourful array of soft, hard, fresh and blue varieties. She had no trouble selling cakes – big trays of apple cakes, vanilla slices and iced buns that were always gone by the end of the week – and as Christmas approached they added biscuits, chocolates and all the accessories that went with Christmas parties, like serviettes, cups and paper plates, to their stock lists. Greg, Kaysie and Chic all helped out sometimes too – Greg, in particular, was always happy to sample anything that might be going begging, and Chic often volunteered to take a shift with Jack so that Marge could have a rest. She loved the time working with her father, and the two of them spent a lot of time talking about sales, recommendations, and revenue building ideas.

They had plenty of regular customers, and it didn't take long before they got to know them and looked forward to them coming in and having a chat. There were some characters too, including a doctor who tried to get a refund for unused serviettes, and a young tradesman who tried to blame Chic because he'd slopped his pie down his shirt. On the whole, though, they enjoyed meeting people each day, and Jack in particular loved talking and chatting to the customers, just as he had done in his early years as a purchaser for the wool and skin shop. They even had a visitor from Murtoa one day, and he and Jack enjoyed a lovely reminiscence for nearly an hour before Marge had to politely point him back to the meat counter.

An exciting moment arrived in 1975, when Ron and Denise moved back from Canada and Marge and Jack met their granddaughter for the first time. They were both incredibly excited to see her, and to be active grandparents as much as they could. The small family squeezed in with Marge and Jack to the small house on Young Street while they looked for their own place, and Marge was happy to babysit as much as she could. Belinda was a chatty little girl, already walking and wanting to be involved in everything, and she followed her grandmother everywhere. Marge, for her part, loved having her around and cherished the time getting to know her.

Soon after that they had a stroke of luck when they heard of a property available for rent just behind the deli. They had the news from some friends at their new church, St David's in Burnside, which they'd joined soon after moving into town. They packed themselves up and shifted again, and now could enjoy the double luxuries of more space and a much shorter walk to work. When the shop was quiet Marge could go out the back door, walk past a couple of houses and be home, and Jack could phone her there if business picked up and he needed her to come back. It also meant she could bring him his dinner at a more respectable time, and he could sit and eat it while she looked after the shop. He still brought the books home to add up after work, but at least now it only took him a minute to get home, and he didn't have to eat his dinner at 9 o'clock. The only downside was that he didn't have a garden, but he didn't really have time for gardening anyway.

Running the deli seven days a week infringed on their football time as well, and despite living so close to The Parade, matches were always on Saturday afternoons and therefore they were never free to go and watch – although if it was quiet Jack could at least listen to the match on the radio, and there were several customers who shared his enthusiasm for the club. It was about a year before business finally became steady enough that they were able to afford some extra help, and they enlisted Jack's sister Mary and a local girl who lived around the corner. At last Jack could take Saturday afternoons off and go to watch the football, and he was often joined by Greg, Kaysie, Ron, Denise and Belinda. Marge enjoyed it more now too, especially as Jack had learned to censor his language a bit with a grandchild around. Finally, their loyalty was rewarded in 1975 when the club won its first premiership since the family had been supporting them.

Being able to watch the footy certainly increased their satisfaction with life but since one of them always had to be in the shop, Marge and Jack still weren't able to spend much time together outside work. Jack had his football, and now that they were living close to the city Marge could occasionally treat herself to a show or concert at the Festival Theatre in town. She loved musicals especially, just as she had loved the Hollywood films of the 40s and 50s, and on the nights when she went out she dressed up in one of her best frocks and caught the bus into North Terrace on her own. There she spent a couple of hours transported from her 7-day working week existence to the streets of Paris, the American mid-west or the mountainous slopes of Austria, where she found a delightful and uplifting escape from the repetition of life. After the show Jack picked her up in the car to take her home, and listened patiently as she regaled him with stories of pirates, carousels and children skipping through alpine meadows. When they did spend time together, it was usually on Sunday afternoons with the family, and they did manage to take one holiday, a weekend away leaving Chic in charge of the shop. It was a much needed and appreciated break, and they were pleased, when they returned, to find all their goods intact and no evidence of any wild parties having been held in their absence.

Life in retail was hard work, but it was a real family business and most of their customers were regulars who came because they liked the friendly and familiar service. In turn, it was the regulars they got to know that kept Marge and Jack going. Every now and then they got a complaint or a grumble, and in those cases it was Marge who laid down the law that she'd learnt previously in retail: *the customer is always right.* Jack didn't always agree, and his fiery temper lost them a few customers in the early days, but with Marge's steady influence and the need to keep business he learnt to control it – or at least to disappear out the back until the mood passed, which never took very long. She had a few similar disagreements with Mary who didn't like to be told she was wrong, but Marge insisted it didn't matter either way – the customer was right, whether the staff or management liked it or not (although she did draw the line at refunding the unused serviettes). That was how it was, and most of the time it was a policy that served them well.

There was more exciting news early in 1976 when Ron and Denise became parents again in March, this time to a boy, Shane. Now Marge and Jack had a grandson as well, and he was as different from Belinda as he could have been: shy and quiet, but no less loved by his grandparents and his aunts and uncle. The two of them revelled in the attention from their grandparents – Marge was a doting nanna, although firm when she needed to be, and Jack loved being a grandpa as much as he had enjoyed being a dad. There were often family parties and barbecues, at their house or at Ron and Denise's, and he loved being outside with them. Greg, Kaysie and Chic loved the children as well, and although Marge and Jack didn't have much spare time, they made the most of what there was.

By the beginning of 1977, after Jack and Marge had been working non-stop for nearly three years, the market was beginning to change. Supermarkets were branching out and had begun stocking continental meats and cheeses, directly competing with small businesses like Marge and Jack's Continental Deli. Supermarkets had the added advantage of being able to buy in bulk, which meant they could sell it on more cheaply, and the smaller businesses suffered. They still had their regulars, but they could see where the trend was heading and they decided it was time to move on. They found a buyer for the shop, and thanks to all their hard work and saving, they now had enough money for a deposit on a house.

They found a lovely home, a 30-year-old sandstone fronted bungalow with a bay window and big garden in the nearby suburb of Tranmere, on the corner of Arthur Street and Freeman Avenue. It only had two bedrooms, but it had a nice big kitchen, a dining room with a fireplace, a cosy lounge room and an extension on the back which became a playroom for the grandchildren. It had a long hall with high ceilings, which the children loved running up and down, and a laundry with an extra toilet. The front garden faced onto Arthur Street, with a big lawn and a single, large tree in the middle, and out the back there was a large, paved area running all the way down the side of the house. Next to this was an undercover patio which led to another lawn and a large garage which fitted the car, all Jack's gardening tools and several other bits and pieces they'd picked up along the way. Finally, they had their own place again with plenty of room to spread out and everything they needed – including neighbours – close by. They even had Greg staying with them for a little while, who claimed the back room as a temporary bedroom. Marge and Jack were very pleased that after his travels he had finally finished his school certificate, and then followed it with a financial planning diploma. Showing his father's natural talent for numbers, he did well and was soon earning enough to get his own place in Valley View, leaving Marge and Jack with the house to themselves.

Having the house was wonderful, but they weren't ready – or able – to retire just yet so both of them set about looking for work. Through one of their contacts from the deli, Jack got a factory job for a smallgoods company called Chapman's, one of their old meat and produce suppliers. Unfortunately he wasn't very suited to it – for one thing, he had to drive for an hour each day to get there and then another hour back again, and for another he hated working inside on a production line. He also struggled with the transition from being a business owner to an employee, and didn't get along with his boss at all. Jack was too much of a people person, and often finished his quota of work before the others, at which point his instinct was to go and help someone else. The boss wanted none of that, and insisted he sit by his machine and do nothing for the rest of the shift. It wasn't long before he'd had enough, and he found another job closer to home, through another one of his old deli contacts, in the bottle shop of the Feathers Hotel. This was much more suited to his temperament, as he could serve customers as they drove through, help them load up their cars and chat to them if things weren't too busy. That was how he liked to be – always occupied, but in a companionable sort of way.

Unfortunately, the bottle shop job didn't provide enough hours to fill his time or satisfy the mortgage lenders, so on the side he started up his own gardening business. It began with a couple of friends from church who needed work done on their gardens, but it wasn't long before word got around and he had a steady flow of requests coming in. Finally, he had a routine which included enough work to keep him happy and financially stable, and enough free time to spend with Marge, at the footy, with his family, or in his own precious garden.

Meanwhile, Marge also found work fairly easily. It so happened, the day before they sold the deli, that Marge's old supervisor from John Martin's in Elizabeth walked in, and he recognised her immediately. She mentioned to him that she was planning to apply for a job in the Rundle Mall store, and he was more than happy to offer his name as a reference, but unfortunately they didn't have any openings at that time. The application remained pending, and in the meantime she found a job with Chapman's the smallgoods suppliers – the same one that employed Jack in their factory – in their shop in the Adelaide Central Markets.

If Marge thought things had been busy in the deli, it was nothing to suddenly finding herself in the middle of a busy city market. She only worked two days a week, but they were long days, with little chance for a break as shoppers from all corners of the city streamed in. On Friday mornings Jack dropped her off at 6 on his way up to Nairne, and she was on her feet all day until the market closed at 9 in the evening, when she took the money down to the bank deposit box before Jack picked her up again. On Saturday mornings she was in again by 7, and she worked until the afternoon, and at least at that time she could catch the bus home if Jack was at the footy. It was a tiring time, despite only taking up two days a week, and even Marge had to admit to herself that it was one of the hardest jobs she'd ever had. Fortunately it didn't last long – by November, the Christmas sales season was approaching and John Martin's were finally in need of more staff. She left the market job, and started at the Rundle Mall department store on December 5.

Being back at John Martin's presented a new challenge for Marge – she was not on the sales floor this time, but on the telephone service of the blinds and awnings department. Her job was to pick up incoming phone calls and answer questions about blinds, curtains, awnings and other fittings, and if the caller knew the dimensions of the window she could calculate an estimate of the cost based on what material they wanted, the length of the curtain and what pattern they chose. It was a scary prospect at first, not just because she had to do the calculations and get them right, but also because she had to make recommendations of what she thought was best and hope that the customer would be pleased when they saw it. If they were happy with her estimate and recommendation, then she arranged for a salesman do go out and do a fitting.

She found it a little daunting to begin with, as she felt the pressure of living up to customer expectations – not least because she had taken over the job from a woman who'd been there for twenty years. But she wanted the job badly and she soon got used to it, and when the appreciative comments started coming in it gave her the confidence to keep at it. Her new colleagues took a bit longer to warm to her, no doubt out of loyalty to the previous incumbent, but she was determined to do her best, and as usual Marge's best was more than good enough for her to succeed. With practice and some help from her supervisors she became competent at the job and began to enjoy it, and eventually her sceptical workmates became her close friends. Sometimes in winter, if the phones were quiet, she spent some shifts out on the sales floor, but mostly she sold curtains, and once again she enjoyed the companionship of her colleagues, the satisfaction of being good at doing something she enjoyed and the part-time hours which meant she had time and energy for her home life as well.

Meanwhile, Jack was getting more and more gardening work and eventually reached a point where he felt secure enough to give up the job at the Feather's and garden full time. It suited him perfectly – he was his own boss again, he was getting paid for doing something he loved, and as most of the gardens belonged to friends or friends of friends, he enjoyed the company of everyone he worked for. Most days he was up and off by 8 a.m. and each day Marge packed him his lunch, either a sandwich, leftovers or a pie or sausage roll that she'd made. She tried to get him to eat fruit, but he refused to eat an apple with the skin on it and couldn't be bothered to peel an orange so she gave up on those, but occasionally she packed him a banana and he didn't mind them so much. He spent about two or three hours at each house, tending lawns, pruning roses, planting vegetables, cleaning gutters, and doing whatever else was needed, and he loved it. He spent his days outside as he had always preferred, and though he held himself to high standards and worked hard, not having any external pressure from bosses, opening hours or quotas to fill brought with it a freedom that he had never enjoyed before, not to mention enough energy at the end of the day to actually spend some leisure time with his wife. They only thing they argued about was how much he charged – Marge thought it wasn't enough, but as his clients were mostly pensioners he didn't like to ask for more. So they made do with what he got, along with Marge's wage from John Martin's.

Marge was working three days a week to begin with, and sometimes four or five in busy periods. It was no trouble for her to get into the city on her own, as there was a bus stop right outside the house on Arthur Street, and it dropped her off on Pulteney Street right in the centre of town. From there she only had to walk halfway down Rundle Mall and she was at work. At the end of the day she could enjoy her walk back down the Mall, then cut through the Renaissance Arcade back to Pulteney Street to catch another bus home. She usually got in by around 5 p.m., and Jack was home soon after that. She always cooked dinner which they ate together at the small table in their kitchen, and they spent their weeknight evenings watching television together, something they had never had time to do before.

In the 70s and 80s Australian Television had a lot to offer. In 1975 all television companies switched to colour, and with the addition of SBS in 1980, there were five major channels to choose from. Marge and Jack particularly enjoyed all the game shows, and their favourites were *Pick-a-Box*, *Blankety-Blanks* and later on *Sale of the Century* and *Wheel of Fortune*. On the weekends, if they were home, they had *Hey Hey it's Saturday*, with its hosts Daryl Somers and his puppet sidekick Ossie the Ostrich, and on Sundays there was *Countdown* on ABC with Molly Meldrum, a music television show which launched the careers of several future success stories – including John Farnham, Kylie Minogue, AC/DC and INXS.

There was a lot of drama being produced at the time as well, and some of the most popular shows of the era were American imports such as *Charlie's Angels*, *Laverne and Shirley*, *I Dream of Jeannie* and *Bewitched*. Marge and Jack also enjoyed a number of Australian police and detective dramas that appeared at the time, including *Cop Shop* and *Prisoner*, which was set in a fictional women's prison. In 1985, Channel 10 relaunched the soap opera *Neighbours*,* but they preferred Channel 7's offering *Home and Away*, set in the idyllic seaside town of Summer Bay in New South Wales.

Live sport was now being broadcast regularly as well, including Olympic and Commonwealth Games, horse racing, golf, tennis and cricket. South Australian viewers could also watch the VFL, the only Australian Rules

---

* Neighbours was initially launched in July 1985 by Channel 7, where it struggled for a few months before being cancelled and bought by Channel 10. In July 1987 two million Australians tuned in to see the wedding of Scott and Charlene, played by Kylie Minogue and Jason Donovan. Curiously, the show enjoyed enormous popularity overseas – in comparison, the same episode in the UK drew 20 million viewers a year later.

Football league in the country to rival the local SANFL. Victoria was South Australia's great rival when it came to footy, and each year the State of Origin match between the two states was hotly contested by fans and players alike.

Meanwhile, life at home for Marge and Jack became more peaceful but fuller than ever, and now they finally had the time and energy to enjoy it. Jack tended his garden, adding a vegetable patch at the back and plots around the lawn filled with geraniums, hydrangeas and pansies. The front garden, as a corner plot, had a low stone wall running along two sides of it, and he planted roses all the way around the carefully tended lawn. He spent many hours outside watering and pruning his roses and chatting to whoever wandered past. As the bus stop was right in front of the house, there was always someone going by, and in time Jack got to know most of the people in the neighbourhood. In his vegetable garden he planted zucchinis, radishes and tomatoes, which he tied up with bits of binding twine leftover from old haybales. Hydrangeas surrounded the back lawn, and to these he gave the royal treatment – each summer they were covered in shade cloth to protect them from the searing rays of the sun, then they were carefully pruned and tidied so that in the spring they were bursting with magnificent blooms and the garden was framed with a spectacle of colour.

They were soon on good terms with their next-door neighbours, and only a few weeks after they moved in the neighbours behind them on Freeman Avenue, Ken and Margaret Bellchambers, invited them around for afternoon tea. There they also met their neighbours on the other side, Roma and Clarry Hector, and so began a long friendship between the three households, which continued when Clarry died not long afterwards when he had a heart attack on the top of Ayers Rock. The three households took it in turns to host the others for dinner and card games, and it was a tradition they carried on until Ken died nearly thirty years later.

In 1981 the whole family (with the exception of Denise and Shane, who had chicken pox) travelled back to Victoria for a Stevens family reunion. All eight of Jack's siblings were there, with their partners and many children and grandchildren. It was a wonderful day, a simple picnic in the park full of games, chatting and laughter, and Marge and Jack met a few of their nieces and nephews for the first time. It was a happy carefree day, which turned out to be even more special than they realised, as it was the last time all nine of the Stevens siblings would be together at the same time.

There were 83 family members there that day, which was all a bit overwhelming for Greg's new girlfriend Louise, who had agreed, somewhat apprehensively, to go. She must have had a good impression though, because the following May they were married at Our Lady Queen of Peace church in Payneham. Marge and Jack were delighted with Greg's choice (despite the fact that she and her family supported the rival North Adelaide Football Club), and Jack even forgave the fact that the wedding clashed with a Norwood match. He took a small transistor radio with him so he could get updates, although he must have wondered why he bothered as they lost to Sturt by 27 points.

At least the wedding went as it should have, and later that year Norwood won another premiership, despite the unfortunate loss to Sturt earlier in the year. A couple of months after that, in November (after a very long labour which had the whole family biting their nails), Karleen was born, another granddaughter for Marge and Jack, and when she was followed by a boy, Benjamin, in May 1984, family gatherings became happier and noisier than ever and Marge and Jack's big garden and patio were regularly put to good use.

By this time Marge had been working at John Martin's for five years and had settled into her job well. She was even able to take advantage of some of the perks – as the company was the sponsor of the Adelaide Christmas

Pageant, employees could apply to take part. Marge finally decided to give it a go one year and she was cast as a beauty pageant contestant. She was to walk alongside a beach themed float dressed in a pink and grey knitted swimsuit, a two-piece made in the old-fashioned style with a long top and knee-length shorts. She and the rest of the participants had to arrive in the city by 7 a.m. to have their make-up done, then they gathered to wait in the park across the road before the pageant started at 10. She had packed sandwiches and ate those for breakfast, but was a little surprised to discover that many of her comrades had packed drinks as well and were in rather high spirits by the time the pageant started. Once everyone was ready they took their places and she followed the route through the city, down King William Street and into the store at Rundle Mall, waving back at the thousands of children who lined the streets to see them, full of excitement for the impending arrival of Father Christmas.

She had such a good time doing the pageant that she signed up again the next year, expecting to reprise her role as a beauty queen. Instead, when she went for her costume fitting she discovered that one of her colleagues had swapped her name, and she found herself listed as one of the ugly sisters in the Cinderella Pantomime float. The costume lady offered to change it back, but Marge, unflappable as always, waved her objections aside, saying that if the other lady wanted to be a beauty queen so badly then they may as well let her, since she didn't really mind either way. It was a particularly warm day that year, and she could feel her make up melting off as she marched through the city, waving and smiling at throngs of happy children and hoping they didn't notice an occasional dab at her liquefying face.

By September 1983 Marge had moved to the furniture department and was once again on the sales floor talking directly to customers. She still enjoyed it, but she was getting tired and Chic, who was now running a restaurant in Adelaide, wanted her to come and help out during the days. There was only one problem, and that was that Shane and Belinda desperately wanted to be in the pageant, but Shane wasn't quite old enough yet. So she stayed on another year, and all three of them entered the pageant in 1984. Marge was cast as a clown, so she could wander along as she liked and wave and talk to the children. She stayed at John Martin's for the rest of the Christmas period before resigning her position, and her final day at work was December 21, after working seven years in the same store.

CHAPTER TWELVE

When in Rome

* * *

In the new year she started working for Chic, who was now very busy co-running two restaurants in the city. Denise came and helped as well, while Shane and Belinda were at school, and the two of them spent the mornings cleaning and setting tables for lunch. Marge also helped with administration, paperwork and answering the phones, and Chic found her to be a handy and reliable employee, who only needed to be shown how do things once and then could be left to get on with them. Jack helped out by picking up the laundry every couple of days and getting it washed for her, and both of them enjoyed being part of the team and the business.

Meanwhile, Kaysie was currently living and working overseas, dancing with her partner Brian in Switzerland, so Marge and Jack had inherited her cat, Lune. Marge was desperate to do some travelling herself, but apart from a visit to New Zealand to visit June and her husband Colin, Jack could not be persuaded to leave the country – he liked Australia, he was comfortable with the familiar, and his sense of adventure did not stretch to exotic foods and foreign languages. Besides, he had so much family spread out all over the country that his options for visiting relatives in Australia were virtually unlimited, so why bother travelling overseas?

Chapter Twelve – When in Rome

So Marge had resigned herself to domestic holidays for the time being, but with Kaysie living overseas she wondered if perhaps he could be persuaded that it would be just another visit. She broached the subject carefully one weekend, when Jack was relaxing with a cup of tea, his tongue sticking out of his mouth as he concentrated on the newspaper crossword.

"What about going to visit Kaysie and Brian?" She asked him. "Switzerland is supposed to be very beautiful, and they could show us around."

"The only reason I would go would be to visit Kaysie," was Jack's reply.

That was enough for Marge. She was at the travel agent's on Monday morning, booking them a trip to Europe before he could change his mind.

They arrived in London in the middle of July and on the recommendation of the travel agent they stayed in England for a week. Jack had protested at this unintended expansion of their itinerary, but Marge (and the rest of the family) had insisted on it, and so he submitted, albeit reluctantly. Jim and Eileen's youngest son Louis was living in London at the time, so they planned to meet up with him and see some of the sights of the city.

Even as they arrived at the airport and boarded the plane Jack was convinced that something would go wrong, and all his worst fears were confirmed when they arrived in London and were informed their hotel had been overbooked and didn't have a room for them. He fumed and stomped around the airport and was ready to get straight back on the plane, when the desk clerk suggested that perhaps he might like a cup of tea. Sensing danger, Marge directed him to an empty corner and told him to sit down and be quiet, before he could make any suggestions as to what she could do with the cup of tea. She took over the negotiations with characteristic aplomb, waited while the concierge found them a new and better hotel, and then insisted that they provide the taxi fare as well. So they had a lovely hotel room in the heart of London, which mollified Jack a little bit, but the cup of tea clearly hadn't done its work and as soon as they'd settled in he stomped down to the bar for a drink. To his surprise, the barman presented him with a pint of bubbling, cold beer.

"How did you know?" he asked the barman.

"From your accent," was the reply.

He took a long sip, and as it went down Jack began to feel that a week in London might not be so bad after all.

They saw all the famous sights: Buckingham Palace, the Thames, Piccadilly Circus and Covent Garden. Marge would have loved to have seen a West End show or two, but as Louis was there, they spent the evenings with him, catching up on all the family news and eating in English pubs. From London they took a tour up to the Lake District for a few days, and though the scenery was stunning and the weather was good, the thing that surprised and delighted Jack most was a visit to an English rose garden. He spent several hours wandering around it and gaping at the blooms, marvelling at the fact that a rose could have grown as well in England as it did in Australia. They went to Scotland as well, where even Marge tried the local whisky, because – as she pointed out – when in Rome, one should do as the Romans do. Then they headed back to London and from London they flew on to Switzerland.

They landed in Geneva where Brian had arranged a lovely unit for them close to where he and Kaysie were working. They stayed for almost a month, catching up with their daughter and watching her dance whenever they were home in the evenings. During the days they took several trips out to various towns and villages, some in Switzerland and some just across the borders into France and Germany. They took several rides on cable cars, over the mountains and gorges, and Jack cowered in his seat, as small as he could make himself, while Marge leaned out as far as she could for a better glimpse at the wondrous views beneath them. They tried plenty of cheese and lots of local meats and sampled all the Swiss chocolate. Kaysie took them for a weekend in Paris and they travelled by train across the alps, and spent a couple of wonderful days looking at the Arch of Triumph, the Eiffel Tower and the Champs Elysees. To finish it off, Kaysie took them for dinner and a show at the Moulin Rouge, and so Marge finally got to see a show, combined with a marvellous dinner and a few glasses of cool French wine.

They spent another weekend in Rome, and again Marge was excited to see a new part of the world – especially one she had heard so much about. Italy was a country of food, religion, antiquity and shopping, and she couldn't wait to go exploring. Jack had other ideas, however, as he had heard too many stories about pickpockets, handbag slashing and swindling salesmen to be comfortable in what he saw as a land of noise, traffic and crowds, and wouldn't let Marge into a single shop – at least, not with her handbag. So she didn't do any shopping, but they did spend one day at the Colosseum and another at the Vatican, and even Jack had to admit that it was a grand and majestic place. They spent their final day in Rome going through the Vatican museums, and after several hours marvelling at paintings, sculptures and the famous frescoes of the Sistine Chapel, they realised they were running late to catch their train back to Switzerland that evening. It was an uncomfortable dash back to the hotel, after one taxi driver got them lost and they spent an hour or so wandering the streets of Rome, asking for directions and being sent in every which way in an ever-increasing state of panic and frustration. Finally they found a taxi driver who knew the hotel and they arrived, hot, sticky and dishevelled, to find their cases and things ready for them in the lobby, and their guide waiting to bundle them straight into a taxi to the station. They made the train, thankfully, and despite not having been able to freshen up beforehand, they managed to relax at last.

The scenery was beautiful, and they sat back and enjoyed the view as they journeyed through the rolling hills of Tuscany and Reggio-Emilia and on past the vineyards and lakes of the Veneto. After about an hour, they began to realise that they hadn't had time to grab any supplies for the trip, nor had they had time to eat anything. When the train finally stopped near the border with Switzerland Marge jumped off to buy bottles of water and a snack with the last of their lira, while Jack hopped up and down on the carriage steps convinced that the train was going to leave without her. She made it back in time, and the supplies were very welcome, but there was another unpleasant surprise waiting when the inspector came around and they realised that in the rush to get on the train they hadn't validated their tickets. Jack – ever the nervous traveller – started panicking again, so Marge gave him strict instructions not to say a word when the inspector came around. She put on her most innocent tourist face but unfortunately couldn't get them out of paying a fine – still, it was better than going back to Rome and paying for another night in the hotel. Finally, they were on the move again to Switzerland, and they could look out at the snow-capped Alps and the crystal-clear lakes and rivers knowing that Kaysie and their now-familiar apartment would be waiting for them at the other end.

They made one more trip from Switzerland, and that was to visit Jack's sister Mary in Germany, who was staying with her daughter Pam in a small town in Bavaria called Marktheidenfeld. Unfortunately, while they were still in Switzerland they received the sad news that Jack's brother Jim had passed away in Tasmania, after suffering many years with ill health and heart trouble. It was a sharp blow for Jack, who had been close to his brother his whole life, had worked with him, run a business with him and lived with him several times. They arrived in Germany on Friday August 2, which was the day of Jim's funeral in Tasmania. After having to get up at 4 a.m. in order to catch two trains to get to Marktheidenfeld, Jack was looking and feeling very knocked around by the time he arrived, but being able to spend the day with his sister was a comfort to both of them, and at least they could share their grief.

The next day cheered them up a bit as Pam took them to the nearby town of Rothenburg ob der Tauber, famous for its medieval buildings and its Christmas shop, Kathe Wohlfahrt. Jack waited in a pub while the ladies looked at Christmas decorations, and Marge declared it the most beautiful shop she'd ever been in. Pam cooked them all a Chinese dinner in the evening, which was a happy occasion and a nice change from all the heavy Germanic food.

From there they went back to Geneva for one more week with Kaysie, then they made another, final stop in London on the way home and caught up with Louis again. He was naturally more subdued than when they had first seen him, after the loss of his father, but the presence of his uncle and aunt did at least cheer him up a little bit. From there they flew back to Australia, and although Jack, particularly, was glad to be back on Australian ground, even he had to admit that it had been a wonderful trip. Despite his reservations – which had been many – he had loved seeing Europe and its spectacular scenery, the highlight of which had been the visit to the English rose garden. Marge, of course, had loved every minute of it, and spent many hours looking through the photos afterwards and talking about it to anyone who would listen. It would be a few years before she made it overseas again, but now she had the bug, and she knew in her heart she would be travelling again one day.

Once reality had settled back in Marge went back to work for Chic, and Jack resumed his gardening. There were no more big overseas holidays, however shortly after agreeing that was enough for a while, an opportunity came up to go on a bus trip to Darwin with Jack's former army mates. It was a camping trip, and Marge was nervous about sleeping in a tent, but the opportunity was too good to pass up and she agreed to go. They met in Mildura and travelled north, visiting several of the camps and bases that Jack's unit had been stationed at during the war. Several of them were still there, left just as they had been when hostilities ceased, and Jack had a wonderful time reminiscing with his old friends, and seeing for the first time in forty years the places that held memories of a time that was not a happy one, but nevertheless had forged the characters of, and friendships with, the men he travelled with now. Marge, for her part, felt the sense of comradeship between them, and it was hard not to feel that she knew the men so well already, from hearing Jack talk about them for so many years. She enjoyed getting to know them in person, and she made many enduring friendships with their wives. It was not a luxurious trip (toilet stops involved pulling the coach over on the side of the road and the guide announcing: "ladies to the left, men to the right!") but it gave Marge a glimpse into a period of Jack's life that she hadn't previously known much about. They both had a wonderful time, and Marge felt afterwards that she knew a little more about her husband than she had before.

It was also around this time that they joined the local RSL branch in the nearby suburb of St Morris and began participating in the Anzac Day activities. Most of his former comrades – those who were still alive – were in Victoria where his regiment had been based, but there was usually a Victorian battalion or two represented and so he joined them for the Anzac Day parade, marching through the streets of Adelaide with his medals displayed on his chest. After that he and Marge met the St Morris members at the clubrooms for lunch and reminiscences. When they had time they also went to their monthly meetings, where the men enjoyed a game of billiards and the ladies played cards for five cent pieces. It wasn't the same as seeing his old mates of the 7th AIF, but he kept in touch with them by letter, and in the meantime he enjoyed the company of men who at least understood what it was to have been a serviceman in World War Two.

There was one more holiday after the Mildura trip, a return to New Zealand, and this time, after visiting June and Colin on the north island, they made a further trip to the south island. It was their first time there, and the thing they were most looking forward to was a visit to the fjords of Milford Sound at the very end of their trip. As the tour reached its end, they had a bit of money left over so they decided to splurge and take a scenic flight – how spectacular it would look from the air! But on the day they were due to fly, the weather was bad and all flights were cancelled. They had one more day so they waited to try again, but once again the weather was bad and they couldn't fly – and by now it was too late for them to take the train. They missed out on the fjords, but still they'd had a lovely time, and perhaps they would make it back again one day.

Back in Adelaide, things weren't going well for Chic. Her business partnership had collapsed and she had decided to leave the restaurants, but the hospitality industry in Adelaide was small and she was having a hard time finding another opportunity. Since she was at a loose end, Marge suggested she go away for a few months, so she got in touch with a few friends and one of them offered to have her in Queensland. She left at the beginning of 1992.

At this point Marge decided she'd done enough working, and as she was almost 65 – when she would be eligible for a government pension – she made the decision to fully retire. She had two more grandchildren now – Greg and Louise had another boy, James (named for Greg's uncle Jim) in December 1986, and a girl, Elizabeth, in October 1991 – and being retired meant she would be available to help Louise a bit more if she was needed. She tried to urge Jack to do the same, but he couldn't face the idea of doing nothing – no matter how much Marge insisted that they would find things to do – and anyway he enjoyed the gardening too much to give it up. In the end she convinced him to at least slow down a bit, so he scaled back the gardening until he was only working part time, and his income was supplemented by a small army pension from Veterans' Affairs.

This seemed a fair compromise for Marge, who felt a bit lost at first with all the free time, but she had plenty of friends now who were also retired, so if she wanted to go out during the day she could always find company. One of these was a lady called Joyce, who she knew from John Martin's and who had by coincidence also been a friend of Mary's. Marge and Joyce spent many days together going to lunches and concerts, and they became even closer friends as the years passed until Joyce became a friend to most of the family and was often invited to parties and birthdays.

Marge and Jack did go to the movies sometimes, usually at the Chelsea Theatre on Kensington Road, and of course they still went to the footy on Saturdays. Now they had daughters-in-law and grandchildren with them they took seats in the stands, or brought cushions to sit on the concrete steps behind the goals, and Marge always had her knitting with her, watching the game and clicking away with her needles. In those days they couldn't afford to buy lunch for everyone, and so, as her own mother had done so many years before for picnics and parties, Marge packed sandwiches and whatever cakes or slices she had baked. The grandchildren loved going to the games, especially if it involved sampling pieces of their nanna's famous vanilla slice or chocolate hedgehog. They thrived on the atmosphere of the crowds, cheering when the team played well and never booing, because Grandpa disapproved of that. They had to stifle giggles whenever he lost his temper, but he always let them mark the goals in the match-day Budget magazine and they joined him in full voice when the club song, *A Grand Old Flag*, was played over the loudspeakers. It was a special treat if they were allowed to visit the clubrooms after the match, and it filled them with great pride if he ever let them wear his red and blue hat.

Meanwhile, the game was changing around them. In 1982, the Victorian football club South Melbourne had relocated to Sydney, meaning that there was now a league in Australia with teams in more than one state. In 1987, Brisbane and Perth each added a team to this league, and in 1990 it changed its name to the Australian Football League. In 1991 South Australia added its own team, which combined players from each of the SANFL's nine teams. Now the family had another team to barrack for, and the Adelaide Crows, wearing the state colours of red, yellow and navy blue and coached by the former Glenelg player and State of Origin coach Graham Cornes, played their first match at Football Park on Friday March 22. They beat the visiting Victorian team Hawthorn by 86 points and would go on to finish the season in 9th place – a respectable result for a debut team.

The 1990s were now in full swing and the family continued to grow and spread out. On April 5, 1992 – the day of Marge and Jack's 45th wedding anniversary – Kaysie married Nigel Hamilton in a wedding ceremony that involved all her nieces and nephews (except for 5-month-old Elizabeth who spent the night with Louise's parents). Belinda was a bridesmaid, along with Chic who had flown back from Brisbane, Karleen was the flower girl and Shane, Ben, Jim and Nigel's two boys Damian and Nicholas were ushers. Kaysie and Jack travelled to the church – Marge and Jack's own St David's in Burnside – in an open horse-drawn carriage, Jack clutching a Norwood umbrella to protect his eldest daughter from the drizzling rain. The following year, in November, Kaysie became a mother when her daughter Juliette was born, and as she was now getting plenty of work as a seamstress (a talent inherited, no doubt, from her grandmother) Marge's days once again became filled with looking after a small granddaughter. Family occasions became busier than ever – sometimes they had barbecues at the local park, and sometimes they had parties at Greg and Louise's new house with a swimming pool – but more often than not they gathered at Marge and Jack's house on Arthur Street, where the adults could sit under the vine-covered patio and the children could play on the lawn, in the courtyard, or in their playroom at the back of the house. Marge's cooking became renowned, not for being fancy or exotic, but for being simple, delicious fare made with plenty of love. Her hospitality was boundless, and more than once the family would turn up for a special occasion to find someone they'd never met before – usually a friend of one of the children or perhaps a relative of one of the in-laws – who she'd invited because she'd discovered they were on their own. Joyce was often there, so was Jim and Eileen's daughter Robyn with her own small daughter Kate, and June and Colin's daughter Debbie, who lived in Adelaide for a while with her husband Rex and two small boys, Tom and Sam. Nigel's two boys added to the growing brood of children, and all of them became like extra grandchildren to Marge, who never seemed to run out of love to give.

Jack loved them all too, but they did stretch his patience when it came to running and trampling on his garden. They knew better than to play where his precious plants grew, but sometimes their balls and toys did end up in a flower patch and there was nothing for it but to sneak in and retrieve them when he wasn't looking. Eventually he became fed up with this and dug out some holes in the back lawn where he placed empty food cans so they could play mini golf, and hopefully stay on the lawn. Though this delighted them and kept them entertained for many hours, it didn't entirely keep them out of the plant beds (they were good for hiding in after all) and it was a lucky grandchild who never found themselves crouching behind a hydrangea when the sprinklers suddenly spurted into life! But other than the flower beds Jack was more than happy for his grandchildren to play in his garden, and they loved to be out there with him. They climbed the tree in the front garden, learned to ride their bikes on the large patio, and spent many hours between them pottering behind him, always ready to hold the hose or pass a pair of secateurs. To the children, Nanna and Grandpa's house was a place where they always felt safe and cherished, and though Jack was quick to lose his temper with naughty or opportunistic children, in his usual fashion he was always just as quick to forgive and forget afterwards. It was a house filled with love, and that love had its roots in the deep and unshakeable affection that Marge and Jack felt for each other after almost half a century of battling and surviving together.

CHAPTER THIRTEEN

In Sickness and in Health

***

Life carried on at home and they were content, with Jack gardening part-time and Marge enjoying retirement, going out with her friends and looking after the grandchildren as often as she could. They often made trips interstate to visit their families: Marge's sister Bonny was still living in Horsham, there were trips up to Brisbane to visit Chic, who had ended up staying there and was now running another busy restaurant, and Jack's sister Mary who had also moved from Adelaide up to Queensland. They had enough room for house guests now, which was handy because there were plenty of visits from Eileen and her family who were all down in Tasmania, Debbie and Rex and their boys who were up in Queensland, and various other siblings, nieces and nephews. Jack had only six siblings remaining now, after the third sister, Mabel, died in 1988, so time spent with their families seemed more precious than ever.

Even June and Colin made it over from New Zealand one year, and as a treat they took them down to Victor Harbour one day. Jack was approaching 70 now, and though he kept fit by walking and working outside, he had been complaining for a couple of years about indigestion and was in the habit of carrying Quick-Eze with him everywhere. Walking back along the causeway on this particular day, Jack found himself out of breath and had to stop – something that had never happened in all his years of physical work. The Quick-Eze was no help, so the next day he went to the doctor, who confirmed the problem was his heart. He was sent straight to the Adelaide hospital where he underwent immediate triple bypass surgery.

The surgery went well, and after a week he was sent home for Marge to take care of him. Despite the success of the surgery, the incident had scared Jack, especially as the specialist had advised him that he had probably been only a few days from having a major heart attack which he might not have survived. He was determined to follow doctor's orders, so despite his frustration at not being able to work he spent the summer resting on the couch watching cricket – so much so, that he developed thrombosis in his legs and ended up back in hospital, which frustrated him even more. From then on he determined to regain his fitness and he walked every day, until after a few months he was declared fully recovered and could return to work.

This was a relief to Marge as well – not just from Jack's impatience at being stuck in the house, but because she was waiting to have surgery on an ulcer, something which was causing her severe discomfort but had necessarily been deferred due to Jack's more urgent treatment. Once he was back at work though, Marge was free to have her own operation, and Jack took care of her as she had him, and in time she was back to her cheerful best and life went back to normal.

Sometime early in 1995, Jack began to have issues with his health again and the doctors determined that his cholesterol levels were very high and his major arteries were becoming blocked. He underwent more surgery to have his carotid arteries cleaned out, and once again it was a great success and it looked as though Jack had plenty of years left in him. Then inexplicably, mere weeks after the surgery, he suffered a major stroke and was rushed to hospital once more.

He survived the stroke, to the family's great relief, but lost the use of the right side of his body as well as the ability to speak. Therefore, once the doctors were satisfied that his life was not in danger, he was transferred to the Hampstead Centre in Northfield for rehabilitation. This was a long and difficult process for Jack, who went from being so active and working every day to not being able to walk or speak. Tasks which he had taken for granted before, like eating, dressing or cleaning his teeth, now had to be done for him by somebody else, a nuisance which he found immensely frustrating. For someone who had always enjoyed chatting to people, not being able to talk was deeply infuriating, and as he couldn't hold a pen he couldn't communicate by writing; nor could he do his daily crossword which he had always enjoyed so much. He couldn't go to the footy – although neither the Redlegs nor the Crows were doing very well that year. He could at least watch it on the television at the centre, and although he couldn't articulate what he was thinking, when it came to his opinion on the play or the umpiring he had no trouble making himself understood.

He spent several months at the Hampstead centre, where physiotherapists helped him regain strength in his legs, speech therapists helped him begin to talk again and occupational therapists helped with his cognitive and motor skills. This meant he could do start to do things for himself again, and it helped restore a little of his pride and dignity. He had plenty of visitors too, and that kept his spirits up, especially if they wanted to talk about football or gardening.

Despite the positive outlook, this was an extraordinarily difficult time for Marge. The stroke itself had come as quite a shock, especially since Jack had been so careful of his health after the heart surgery, and unlike the heart trouble there was no history of strokes in his family. Doctors and therapists gave her every reason to hope he would recover, but she could never stop worrying about him, and now for the first time in her life she found herself living alone in a big house, with an even bigger garden. The family rallied around her and helped her to look after the place, so that she could tell him, truthfully, that she was managing and that everything at home was fine.

She visited him every day, catching a bus into town and then another one out to Hampstead Road, in the suburbs north of the city. She spent the day with him, chatting away even though he couldn't chat back, watching television with him – perhaps one of their favourite game shows – or just sitting beside him knitting away, so the reassuring 'click clack' of the needles filled the room with their familiar sound.

The rest of the family pitched in and took turns to drive her home at the end of the day so she didn't have to catch another two buses. Sometimes it was Greg or Ron, picking her up after work, sometimes it was Kaysie, Denise or Louise, who came by after the school run, sometimes with the grandchildren so they could say hello. Her friends from church often volunteered and even Louise's parents, Maureen and Dinty, chipped in on some days. This made a huge difference to Marge, who was always tired at the end of the day, yet still had dinner to make and housework waiting for her when she got home. She also knew that Jack would be anxious about his garden, and she was determined that when he came home he would find it, if not in perfect condition, at least in some state of having been maintained. Greg and Ron helped with pruning and mowing, but she took the watering on herself, and every evening when she got home she went around the whole garden with the hose or the watering can, keeping his pot plants and his precious roses alive. Then she made herself some dinner and went to bed, ready to do it all the next day. It was exhausting – the only time in her life when she found herself losing weight – but she didn't begrudge or resent it, in fact she didn't think much about it at all, because she knew how much the garden meant to Jack, and was grateful just to have him with her and to be able to see him every day.

After several months of therapy Jack had learned to walk by stepping on his left leg and pulling his right leg along behind him. It was more of a shuffle, but he could move himself without help and that made a massive difference to his morale. He still had trouble with his speech, but he learned to communicate with gestures and sounds, and he could dress and feed himself and take himself to the bathroom, and gradually his confidence returned. He refused to give up on his exercises, even when they made him grit his teeth in frustration, and day after day Marge marvelled at his resilience and determination. Slowly he learned to use his left hand to do things like brush his teeth and comb his hair, and eventually Marge felt reassured enough to spend one day a week at home, so she could rest, catch up on her housework or see her friends.

Jack continued to improve and once the specialists were satisfied that either he or Marge could take care of all his necessary functions, he was able to spend some days at home. He travelled by taxi from the centre in the morning, and then Marge saw him into another taxi at the end of the day. It was wonderful to have him home – they could eat together in their familiar kitchen, watch television in their own lounge and have the family over for lunches and birthday parties. Most importantly, Jack was reassured that his garden was being looked after in his absence. Finally, after several months of therapy and rehabilitation, he was given the all-clear to come home, and Marge was thrilled to have him back. He was home in time for Christmas that year, and even more crucially he was home for Chic's wedding three days later.

Chic met Guy in Queensland and when she brought him down to meet the family he fitted in immediately, almost, the family thought, as if he'd always been there. Marge and Jack were delighted to hear of their engagement, and even more thrilled that they wanted to hold an informal ceremony in their garden, if they wouldn't mind. For Jack there was no bigger compliment to his garden, and it was a lovely, warm December day. All the guests gathered on the back lawn facing a small canopy that had been set up next to the outdoor patio (the mini golf holes were all covered up), and this time it was the youngest grandchildren, Elizabeth and Juliette, who had the honour of being flower girls. Juliette, at only two years old, fell asleep in the play room and missed the ceremony, so it was four-year-old Elizabeth who led the way from the house to the garden, sprinkling rose petals as Chic walked behind with Jack, holding on to his good arm and bursting with happiness. Jack took his seat next to Marge and they gave their blessing, Guy's best man sang a heartfelt rendition of Louis Armstrong's *What a Wonderful World* which had most of the guests in tears, and the party carried on with food and dancing into the night. To complete Chic's happiness, she was able to have a dance with her dad, an occasion made all the more poignant by the fact that at one time she had wondered if he'd even be there.

After the wedding, life settled down again and Marge and Jack found new ways to manage – happy, despite the difficulties of Jack's condition, to be home together again. Jack still had physiotherapy and other appointments at the Hampstead Centre, and if none of the family could drive him he took taxis. Eventually he improved so much that Marge felt comfortable leaving him at home, so she was able to go out and see friends or go shopping, which helped to make life feel normal again. On the days when they both went out he was sometimes home before she was, so she'd leave him a banana or some other snack to keep him going until she got home.

They were able to resume many of their previous engagements and hobbies at this time, which cheered them both up immensely. Their friends from church took it in turns to pick them up on Sunday mornings, and an RSL friend came and picked them up once a month for their meetings at the clubrooms. Even though he had never wanted to talk about it much, spending time with others who had lived through the war was a great comfort to Jack, and being able to make these meetings meant a great deal to him. As a special surprise, Marge arranged for him to travel to Melbourne for Anzac Day that year, so that he could march with his own battalion at last. They stayed with his sister Jean for a few days, and as he couldn't walk very far he was driven in a jeep through the streets of Melbourne in the company of his old mates, many of whom he hadn't seen since he was discharged from service in 1945. It was an immensely emotional day for both of them, as Jack waved from the jeep and Marge and Jean waved from the side lines, before joining the local RSL for lunch afterwards. Jack couldn't contribute much to the conversation, but he was there as they shared their memories and relived the old times, remembering fallen comrades and perhaps reminding each other of the times they wrestled each other for fun or put on silly concerts in the middle of the jungle. It was a tiring trip for Marge, getting him to and from Melbourne, but worth every effort, because she could see how much it meant to him to see his friends again at last.

Over time his confidence returned, and apparently so did his penchant for overestimating his capabilities. Marge came home one day to find him out in the garden, grinning from ear to ear attempting to start the lawn mower. There were some stern words exchanged – at least from her side – and some indignant gestures from Jack's, and in the end they agreed that he would only use the lawnmower if someone else was home. Another time she found him retrieving the ladder from under a pile of junk in the garage, determined that he was going to get up and clean the gutters. This time she put her foot down, and insisted that under no circumstances was he to be going up a ladder. He could see she meant business, so he gestured that she should go up – after all, the gutters had to be cleaned. But no, she wasn't going up, in fact there would be no going up any ladders of any kind by anyone. The gutters would be fine as they were, until Greg or Ron could come and do them. And just to be sure he got the message, she declared that if she saw him getting out the ladder again it would be packed off to Greg's place. Finally he admitted defeat, and he didn't try to use the ladder again.

He was, at least, able to look after his garden, and as his fitness improved he could do more and more. He could hold a hose to do the watering, he could mow the lawn – when Marge was home – and he could prune his roses. Marge wheeled out her laundry basket on its old trolley for him to put weeds in when he was weeding, and it was light enough for him to push it back around the house. He had plenty of company – he was followed around the garden by Lune the cat's successor, Snowy, who'd been inherited from Ron and Denise, and whenever he was out the front people walked past as they always had and he waved to them, listened to how they were doing, and felt like he was talking to them. Being able to garden made him happy, and it kept him going.

He and Marge found ways to communicate, and although he never fully regained his speech he did manage to say her name. Having a conversation often involved a lot of pointing, and Marge asking a lot of questions to which he would nod or shake his head, and they got used to getting along in that way. Jack resumed his membership at Heartbeat, a charity he had joined after his heart operation, and through them he went on visits to heart patients in hospitals and tried to cheer them up as best he could. He helped Marge to raise money by selling lamingtons at a bake sale, and he was still able to do all the maths and money counting that she wasn't confident with. Lots of things still frustrated him, but he was determined to do as much as he could and didn't want to miss out on anything. He got fitter and stronger each day, and gradually the family began to accept that this was how life was now.

Soon it was 1997, and a special occasion was approaching. April 5 would be Marge and Jack's 50th wedding anniversary, and May would see Jack's 75th and Marge's 70th birthdays. A big, joint celebration was planned – so big, in fact, that it took place in two parts. On a sunny afternoon in April, Marge and Jack held a garden party for all their friends and many close acquaintances, from church friends to neighbours to old colleagues, and it was a wonderful, happy day sitting outside on Jack's patio with all the people they had gathered over their long and varied lives – some they'd known for only a few years, some they'd known for decades, all together and all equally welcome.

This was followed a couple of weeks later by an even bigger celebration for the family and close friends, up at Greg and Louise's new house, which had a large outdoor entertaining area. A marquee was set up in the courtyard, which was a good thing because it rained all day, and the children got involved by making signs to point guests in the direction of the amenities. Marge and Jack's many siblings and their families had all been invited and several were coming, and they started arriving in the week before the party, with more trickling in every day, creating a kind of carnival atmosphere for days before the party even started. Bonny, Freddie and Yvonne came over from Horsham, Jack's sister Jess came over from Geelong with her daughter Lois and her son-in-law Don, and Jim and Eileen's eldest, Glenn, came over with his wife Sandy.

On the day of the party it was all hands on deck to get ready. Louise, with the help of Karleen and Beth, spent the day in the kitchen getting nibbles and drinks ready and Ben and Jim helped Greg and Glenn set up a bar in an old and currently untenanted bird cage. Furniture, toys and sports equipment were pushed back, trellis tables and chairs unpacked, and decorations put up. Finally, it was time to change and for the party to begin.

Most of the guests arrived on a bus which had been arranged to pick up Marge, Jack, and all the guests staying in or near the city. There was music and dancing, and although Jack couldn't join in, he sat and watched with pride at this gathering of all the people he held dear, representing a life that had spanned many decades, had been lived in many states and withstood many ups and downs. He and Marge had been through many changes and many difficult times together, but their families had been constant throughout, by their sides as they had been for them. To have them all there together for this special occasion was, to them, an honour and a privilege, and they knew that they were lucky to have got there.

The party was a blast from start to finish. There were the usual speeches, cake cutting, a mountain of cards and gifts, and as a special treat someone had arranged for a bagpiper to come and play. It was the only time in the night there was quiet, and a hush settled around the guests as they heard him draw breath a second before the pipes burst into sound. The stirring notes of *Scotland the Brave* rang around the house and the marquee, followed by *Amazing Grace* and *Waltzing Matilda*. There was barely a dry eye anywhere – Greg's red tartan handkerchief made several appearances, and each pause of the pipes was punctuated by several sniffles. Even stoic, steady Marge's eyes were glistening.

After that the dancing continued – there was even a very decent attempt at the Macarena made by most of the older generation – until the bus returned to pick up the guests of honour and those others who had also arrived that way. It had been a wonderful night. Marge and Jack were bursting with pride and happiness, but they were also very tired, and were glad to get home to bed. The next day they gathered again at Greg and Louise's for a family barbecue, and those who could helped to pack up the tables, chairs and marquee while the children volunteered to help open the presents. They farewelled all the interstate guests, and although there was an inevitable feeling of sadness that it was all over, they were on a high for several days, reliving their favourite moments, looking at the photos and making their way through all the gifts. They had plenty to look forward to as well – friends still came to visit, the grandchildren were around most weekends and to top things off, both Norwood and the Crows were playing well that year, and each looked as though they would make the finals. All in all, their outlook was good.

Soon after the party, Jack's health took a sudden turn for the worse. He became much weaker, and he was readmitted to hospital where he was diagnosed with advanced lung cancer. He was put on medication and his condition stabilised, until he was well enough to return home to Marge's care. He was losing strength now, and was unable to walk himself around the house, so Marge learned to help him get in and out of a wheelchair, and to push him around the house so that he could keep her company with whatever she was doing.

The two months that followed were some of the toughest but most precious of their life. Never had their promise to love one another in sickness and in health been more pertinent, as Marge cared for Jack as much as she could, and Jack, who'd always been so busy and active, fought frustration with his failing body. They had a nurse come each day to help with the things Marge couldn't do, but she was at least still able to cook for him and help him eat, chat to him while she did her chores or wheel him out to the garden where he felt most relaxed.

As his health declined it became harder and harder for Marge to care for him. It was becoming more difficult to help him from the chair to the bed and he often fell, and when that happened there was nothing for it but to wait until a nurse could come and help him back up. Nights were difficult, though sometimes the nurse stayed so that Marge could get some sleep, but it was not enough to stave off the fatigue and exhaustion that had become synonymous with daily life. She also began to notice that his mind was not as sharp as it used to be, and he became muddled and uncoordinated at times. The doctors suspected the cancer had spread to his brain, but they decided – and Marge agreed – that it was pointless to subject Jack to more testing at this stage.

The nurses urged Marge to admit Jack into hospice care, but she was reluctant to let him go – difficult as it was to have him home, that was where she felt he belonged. But things were getting harder and harder for her to manage, she was struggling with the house and garden, and so she made the inevitable but agonising decision to let him go. She spoke to him about it, and believed he understood, and though he was upset about it he agreed to go. He was admitted to the Mary Potter Hospice in North Adelaide, where he was entitled to a private room on account of his being a returned veteran. This didn't suit him at all though, as he'd always enjoyed the company of others, and Marge begged them to put him in a ward where he could see what was going on. She visited him every day, as did various members of his family, but it was a waiting game now, and she did her best to be cheerful, sitting by his side as she always had, chatting or knitting or both, and she hoped the familiar sounds of her voice and the clicking needles would be a comfort to him. On Saturday, July 26, less than three months after they had celebrated their golden wedding anniversary, he died at the hospice with Kaysie, Chic and his church minister by his side.

The funeral was held at St David's church in Burnside, where they had been part of the community for more than twenty years, and his ashes were interred in the churchyard outside. It was a surreal time for Marge, who was fighting not only grief but exhaustion as well. She smiled and thanked the numerous friends and acquaintances who came to pay their respects, but it was as though a haze had descended and she went through the motions, barely aware of who was there or what was happening. Her family surrounded her and helped her at home, and at last she could take some time to rest, and to sleep, and to come to terms with her new situation.

It was a sad ending to a long chapter in Marge's life, and the family's as well, but there was a happy footnote. A month after Jack passed away the Adelaide Crows won their first AFL premiership, beating St Kilda by 31 points in the Grand Final at the MCG. Just a week later, Norwood won the SANFL premiership, beating Port Adelaide by a massive 73 points. Most of the family was there to see it, and as the final siren sounded it was hard not to feel that Jack was there in spirit, cheering on his beloved Redlegs and nodding his approval at having handed their arch rivals such a whopping and humiliating defeat. It was a worthy conclusion to a lifetime of faithful barracking, and as the strains of *A Grand Old Flag* rang out around Football Park his loved ones sang along with extra gusto, and each one felt as though they were singing it for Jack.

CHAPTER FOURTEEN

The Things That Really Matter

* * *

Once things had settled down it was time for Marge to make some tough decisions. She loved the house on Arthur Street, but it was a big place to keep clean and the garden was just too much for her to cope with on her own – and she couldn't stand watching it wither away. She decided it was time to downsize, and the family supported her decision. She kept up the watering and pruning to keep the garden looking its best, Greg and Ron helped her clear the garage of all the bits and pieces of tools, materials and equipment that Jack had accumulated over the years, and the grandchildren helped set up a garage sale and made some pocket money in the process. After several trailer loads of junk and detritus had gone to the tip, what was left was packed and tidied up, the house was spruced up and by early 1998 it was ready to go on the market.

One Saturday morning in April Marge and the family waited anxiously in the kitchen as the buyers gathered outside. They could hear the auctioneer's voice as the price went slowly up and up, until finally they heard the sound of applause which meant the house had been sold. Marge was overjoyed when the estate agent came in to confirm the house had sold, for slightly more than she had hoped for. Now she could start making a new plan.

She looked around at several small units and found one she liked not far away in Tusmore Avenue, just off Greenhill Road. It was a perfect spot – close enough that she could go to the same shops, greengrocers and hairdressers if she wanted to, she could keep in touch with her old neighbours and most importantly she could walk to church, only 15 minutes up the road. It was the fifth in a block of six units, so she was far enough from the road for it to be quiet, but close enough for everything to be accessible.

It was a small but spacious unit and she loved it. It had two bedrooms, a small kitchen with room for a small table and a lounge room where she could watch TV or entertain guests. There was a separate laundry which led out into a small courtyard garden, where she had a pair of outdoor tables, a small shed and a row of plants along the fence. There was also a front porch where Marge could sit and have her morning coffee, next to a large lawn area which was shared by all the units. She brought several of Jack's plants with her, in their heavy white ceramic pots, and these she placed around the front and at the back of the unit, so a little bit of Jack's garden was there every time she went outside. She settled in quickly – with all her favourite things and the family around her all the time, it soon became just as much like home as the old house had been.

The move was tiring though, especially with everything that had come before it, and so Marge took a little time to recuperate. She got to know her new neighbours, but without Jack to care for or a house to pack up, she found herself with a lot of spare time and not much to do with it. It was her friend Joyce who finally coaxed her out, and took her to shows, lunches and concerts, sometimes in the city or at the nearby Chelsea Theatre. There was a bus stop around the corner on Greenhill Road that could take her into town in one trip, and Joyce was there, almost every day to begin with, giving her a nudge and encouraging her to get out.

Chapter Fourteen – The Things That Really Matter

Marge joined several clubs and societies in that time too. She was still a member of the RSL in St Morris and she joined the War Widows Guild, where she found not only a way to be of service but the support and companionship of other women in her situation. She also joined Legacy, a charity supporting the families of servicemen and women who are killed or disabled as a result of their military service. (She would end up spending two years as president and then another six as secretary, during which time her main job was to organise the guest speakers.) Through Legacy she joined a group called 'Walk & Talk', which ran guided walks around some of the city's landmarks, such as the museum, library or war memorial. Sometimes they went further afield, to places like Cleland Wildlife Park or the docks down at Port Adelaide, and so they took a coach. Eager to learn new things, she listened with interest to everything the guides had to say. Somehow, the walks were always organised so that they finished at lunch time, so the group could go and eat together at a café or pub, and she made many new friends that way.

She volunteered at the church as well, taking her turn on some Sunday mornings to serve tea and toast after the service, and she joined the roster for church cleaning. She was quite happy polishing all the brass – the job she had preferred when she was a girl and had avoided the cooking – and she cleaned the pews by sitting on a cloth and shuffling along on her bottom while she wiped the back of the row in front. They had a sewing group as well which met every other Wednesday (fortunately they included knitting as a form of the craft) and election days and church fetes were always an opportunity to sell their handiwork and raise money for the church and various charities. Through the church Marge found a volunteer job at their Anglicare charity shop in North Adelaide, and once a month she volunteered at the Red Cross clinic, serving tea and biscuits to pep up donors who had just given blood.

All of this was enough to keep her pretty busy, but of course she still saw plenty of the family too. Marge's unit became the new family gathering place, and the small patio was often packed full of children and grandchildren, whenever there was a birthday or when someone interstate came to visit. Her Friday nights and Saturday mornings were dedicated to looking after Juliette, and of course they all carried on going to the footy to see Norwood and the Crows. The stadiums were modernizing now, with the installation of bigger and better lighting, so games weren't limited to Saturday afternoons – it was a nice change going on a Friday or Saturday evening, and there was cause for celebration in September 1998 when the Crows won the AFL Premiership for the second year in a row. Marge continued her visits to Chic in Queensland every winter, and Belinda had moved to Melbourne so she extended her Horsham trips to include a few days in the state capital. She made it over to Tasmania from time to time to visit Eileen and her family down there, and Marge and Bonny were able to make a final visit to their sister Shirley, who died in a nursing home in Ararat in 2005.

All in all, Marge was happy in her unit. She missed Jack, and though there were plenty of painful reminders and sad moments, there were also times when happy memories came back to her, perhaps when she was sitting on a bus or reading something in the paper, and she had to smile in spite of herself. She kept busy, and with family all around her she had plenty to look forward to. There was just one thing that was niggling away at her, and that was how much of the world she hadn't yet seen. Although Jack had enjoyed their overseas trip he had never shown any inclination to take another one – now Marge had the opportunity to travel further afield, and she decided it was time to take it.

She booked a trip to Canada and Alaska with her sister-in-law Gwen, who was also recently widowed after Jack's younger brother Ivan passed away in May 2000. Greg bought her a small digital camera to take with her and advised her to do everything she could, and she said she would, nervous though she was about travelling without Jack. A few days later her fear had turned to wonder as she and Gwen sped along the Rocky Mountains from Victoria in Canada to Ketchikan in Alaska, gawping at the deep blues and greens of the lakes and the enormous height of the trees from the comfort of her train compartment. Marge was fascinated by all the small villages along the way, with their wooden walkways and colourful houses, and when the tour company asked who would like to take a helicopter ride over the mountains to see the huskies she signed up immediately, and it didn't take long to convince Gwen to go too. Feeling a bit like James Bond they flew up and over the snow-clad mountains, and when the driver of their dog sled asked for volunteers to have a go, of course she raised her hand. She'd never driven a car in her life (apart from the one failed driving lesson), but she felt the thrill of adventure as she held the reins of the sled, and the huskies pulled her and her companions over the glistening white snow. They were under strict orders from the guides that day not to leave any rubbish behind, not to take any sweets in wrappers or even get out a tissue, and their vigilance was evident – the mountainside was pristine, the air clear, and the view spectacular. She returned home with some fantastic memories, as well as some decent photos she'd taken on her small camera. But perhaps more importantly, she came back with the knowledge that the world was vast, and fascinating, and there was nothing stopping her from seeing more of it if she wanted to.

In 2007 she celebrated her 80th birthday with another party at Greg and Louise's place, and she chose a Roaring 20s theme in honour of the decade of her birth. As in the previous party they had a marquee set up, and once again it was good thing because it rained for most of the day and all night. That didn't dampen anyone's spirits though, and her friends and family once again came pouring in from all over the country, dressed up in the spirit of the theme. Marge herself dressed up in a flapper dress complete with long gloves, a sequined head band and a bright red feather boa, and led the dancing with a riotous conga all around the marquee – and she was the last one still on the dance floor at 2 a.m. when most of the guests had gone home. As always it was a party just as she liked it – surrounded by the friends and family who represented the many stages of her life, lots of eating, drinking and chatting, and of course plenty of dancing.

As a treat for her special birthday, Chic and Guy offered to take Marge overseas anywhere she wanted to go. They were somewhat surprised when she suggested Antarctica – it's not known for its shopping or night life, after all – but perhaps she remembered the simple beauty of the Alaskan snow, or perhaps she wanted to go somewhere that was a bit unusual. One thing was certain – she definitely wanted to see some penguins.

To get to Antarctica they had to go to South America first, so they decided to do a tour there as well. They saw mountains and waterfalls, great cities and small villages all swarming with people, and Marge marvelled at the variety and colours she saw everywhere she looked. She loved exploring the market stalls, where men sat knitting and women weaved, and there were bolts of wool in every colour she could imagine and twenty different kinds of corn on the cob. They travelled up to Peru to Machu Picchu, and took the train as far as they could before walking up to view the ruins. When she'd gone as far as she could she stopped and watched as a mist came in, shrouding the ancient city in even more magic and mystery, before heading back down to a normal altitude again.

They spent New Year's Eve in Rio de Janeiro, where in the late afternoon they went for a stroll along the beach and found every shop window and market stall filled with gladioli. When they asked about it, they discovered that it's a traditional New Year's offering to the sea goddess Yemanja, and that everyone always dressed in white for the occasion. So when they got back to their hotel they changed into whatever white clothes they had before heading up to the roof, where the pool had been converted to a dance floor and stalls had been set up selling street food and drinks. They danced the night away on the roof of the hotel, feeling much safer here than on the streets below, where seven million people had crammed onto the beach and the surrounding area. From their vantage point they could see a flotilla out in the bay, and the firework display, and at midnight they watched as all the people along the beach flung gladioli out into the sea, thanking Yemanja for the blessings of the previous year. Chic and Marge watched and danced until the early hours of the new year, and the beats and rhythms of the heady Latin music carried on long into the night.

From Rio they travelled down to Ushuaia at the southern end of the continent, where they boarded a boat down to Antarctica. It was a Russian research vessel but there were about 90 paying passengers on board – in the few days it took to reach the southern continent they got to know several of them, and they all cheered together when the announcement came over the loud speaker that they'd crossed the Antarctic Circle at 66 and half degrees latitude. Once they reached the continent they stayed for several days, and on each day they were taken out onto the ice. After breakfast they got dressed into thermals, woollen jumpers, a thick down jacket, waterproof trousers and another waterproof and windproof jacket, two pairs of gloves, scarves, woolly hats, wellington boots and as many pairs of socks as they could get on. Once they were dressed they went straight out on deck before they overheated under all the layers, and from there they were loaded on to smaller boats which took them to the shore.

Walking on Antarctica was everything Marge had imagined and more. She was a little scared the first time, climbing down the ladder on the side of the ship and jumping into the bobbing Zeppelin – a small, inflatable boat – but she did it anyway and it wasn't long before she was taking it in her stride. They spent several days exploring different areas of the continent, walking along the icy paths and once or twice visiting small settlements on dry land. She got her wish – she saw thousands of penguins, and spent a great deal of time moving aside and waiting for them to file past, waddling and flapping in their funny way, some of them still with their soft downy feathers. She never tired of watching them, or got sick of having to move, even when she stepped off the path one time and found herself waist deep in a snow drift. Chic tried to help her out and ended up in it herself, and Guy shook his head while he waited for their guides to come and fish them out.

Just as fascinating as the penguins was the ice itself, rising up out of the ocean with its enormous mirror-like facade. No matter how much she looked at it Marge couldn't get over the range of colours in it – soft pinks and blues, turquoise greens, all the colours of the rainbow shining and glistening in the sun. Sometimes when they were in the small boats the guides turned off the engines so they could hear the ice crackling, and as she sat there, bobbing in the Antarctic ocean and looking over the vast whiteness, silent except for the soft creaking of the ice and the gentle lapping of the water, she was filled with wonder at the immensity and beauty of the earth.

Returning home in early 2008, things became a little tough for a while as her brother Freddie and her good friend Pat Davis both became very ill. Conveniently they were both living in Geelong, so Marge stayed with her sister-in-law Jess and visited them both each day, one in the morning and one in the afternoon. They died within days of each other, in June, and after the two funerals Marge returned home for a much-needed rest.

A couple of years later Chic offered to take Marge to Egypt and South Africa, and Guy didn't want to miss out, so once again the three of them set off for adventures in distant lands. They started in South Africa, where they

Chapter Fourteen – The Things That Really Matter

spent a couple of days in Cape Town before heading out on safari. They took a train to Zimbabwe and the Victoria Falls before stopping at Kruger National Park, where Marge was amazed to have her own enormous cabin with its own private swimming pool. She was afraid to use it though, having heard too many stories about hippos and crocodiles out in the wild, so she settled for soaking in the large, claw-footed bath instead. They went out on safari every day, sitting in the back of the open top jeep spotting tall giraffes, wandering wildebeest, herds of zebra and several big cats relaxing on the dusty earth. At times she felt scared, heading out into the desert with nothing between themselves and any predators that may be lurking in the undergrowth, but it wasn't enough to stop her from going, and she trusted the driver and the guards who accompanied them. The guides always packed a hamper and if they went out in the morning they stopped for tea and coffee, and in the evenings they had wine and nibbles. It was surreal but wonderful, sitting in the back of the jeep in the warm evening, sipping on a crisp South African sauvignon as herds of elephants sauntered by and the baobab trees became silhouettes against the setting sun.

From there the three of them flew up to Egypt, and it so happened that Marge's granddaughter Karleen was there too, just finishing a tour of her own. They stayed at the famous Mena House Hotel, which sat in the shadow of the great pyramids and was recognisable from its appearance in several old movies, and Karleen was there to greet them when they arrived, waving from the hotel balcony as they drove up in their jeep. They spent a fascinating few days exploring Cairo, from shopping in the bustling markets to venturing into the pyramids at Saqqara – the guide, sensing that Marge was nervous about it, reassured her he would be right behind her to catch her if she slipped in the darkness, so down she went, and came out grinning from ear to ear stating proudly that she'd been inside a pyramid. They only thing that scared her after that was the camel ride that Karleen urged her to go on, and she held on for dear life as the creature lurched up onto its long legs, carried her around the complex and then lurched back down again. They saw the Sphinx, and the many treasures of the Egyptian museum – including the mask of Tutankhamun – but by far the most awe-inspiring thing was the great pyramids of Giza. She walked right up to them and placed her hands on the great carved stones, gazing up in wonder at the size and scale and marvelling at the ingenuity of such an ancient civilization.

From there Karleen left them to fly to Adelaide and they carried on through Egypt, where they explored the vast temple complex at Karnak, the ancient tombs in the Valley of the Kings and the engineering marvel that is the twin temples of Abu Simbel. They spent Christmas Day at the town of Saint Catherine at Mount Sinai – the site in the Old Testament where Moses encounters the burning bush and receives the Ten Commandments – and their Christmas breakfast was a boiled egg and a tub of yoghurt.

They returned from Africa in time for the new year, and Marge settled back into her busy but familiar routine. By now she had been 14 years in her unit, and she was starting to feel that it might be time to move on. She still loved the space, and her little garden, and the location near the shops and bus stops, but it was becoming expensive, and several of the original owners had moved out and been replaced by a series of tenants, so she no longer had a feeling of community around her. Once again she went through all her things and packed up what she wanted to keep, sold the unit, and moved into an apartment in a small estate run by the War Widows Guild. It wasn't far away – only a few kilometres up the road in Rose Park – so she could still go to the same church, use the same shops and go and watch Norwood at The Parade, and now she had a community of women around her and support close at hand should she need it. She felt safe and secure there, and carried on being busy, attending meetings, going shopping and watching shows and movies. Friends and relatives popped in all the time, and her unit, though smaller, continued to be the happy, welcoming family hub that Marge's home had always been.

By now Marge felt that she had seen quite a bit of the world, but far from making her feel that she'd seen enough, it only made her want to see more. She'd never been to Asia, so she and Chic took a trip to Singapore and Thailand, where they went to see the infamous bridge over the River Kwai, on the border with Myanmar. They already knew the story of its construction – how the Japanese forced allied prisoners to build it during the second world war, in appalling conditions which caused many of them to die from disease and starvation – but seeing it for themselves was something entirely different and made them realise how lucky they were to live in Australia, especially for Marge who had lived through the war and come out relatively unscathed.

It was a sobering visit, but they had some fun afterwards by taking a ride in a tuk tuk (which they had to extricate themselves from when the driver insisted on taking them to his friend's hotel) and visiting the famous Raffles Hotel, built at the end of the 19th century during the colonial era. At the time it was known as the grandest and most luxurious hotel for miles around, and many a foreign dignitary – not to mention Rudyard Kipling himself – was entertained in its vast renaissance-style rooms and extended verandas. It was even the first hotel in the region to have electric light and ceiling fans, a welcome addition in the hot and humid climate. It's still one of the most exclusive hotels in the area, and famous for its iconic cocktail, the Singapore Sling. Marge and Chic were tempted to try one, but it was a very hot and humid day, and at $30 each they decided that it would be better, on the whole, to give it a miss. They settled on buying themselves a mug each instead, which cost about the same but at least they could take it with them.

They went to dinner and several shows at the restaurants in Thailand, and Marge marvelled at how beautiful the women were, until Chic pointed out that they were, in fact, men. Unflappable as always Marge just shrugged and said, "Oh, well, don't they do themselves up well!"

In March 2012 Marge received the sad news that her sister-in-law Eileen, who'd been there for Marge through so much of her early married life, had passed away. She made another trip down to Tasmania for the funeral, but she couldn't say long as she was scheduled to go on her next overseas trip in April. Her 85th birthday was approaching, and as it coincided with Kaysie's 60th and Chic's 55th, they decided to make a girls' trip of it and go to Las Vegas. They were joined by Sandra, the widow of Jim and Eileen's eldest son Glenn who had passed away a couple of years before. By a nice coincidence, that year was Sandra's 65th birthday, so it was celebrations all round as they shopped in the mornings, napped in the afternoons and painted the town in the evenings. For Marge, who had always loved music, theatre and dancing, the holiday was like an extended birthday party, and she loved watching the city come alive in the evenings as they got dressed up to go out. Every night they went to dinner and a show, and in the hotels they marvelled at the opulent foyers, each with its own exotic theme. They took a couple of trips out to see the surrounding country, including a helicopter ride over the Grand Canyon, and an overnight trip to Antelope Canyon. In the morning they were up before the sun, and soon after that they stood in the vast and impressive caverns, marvelling at the colours and shapes of the wind-sculpted rocks that stood still and quiet in the early hours before the tourist buses arrived. For their final evening they went to see Celine Dion in concert, and as they enjoyed supper and wine at the Caesar's Palace restaurant afterwards they all agreed it was the best of the shows they'd seen. In the spirit of the location she played on some of the poker machines, but for Marge it was mostly about the atmosphere, the entertainment, and having a good time with the girls.

Later that year Marge had another chance to go abroad when Karleen, who was back in England again, secured tickets to some football matches at the London Olympics. She flew over in July and set off with Karleen on a road trip that took in the New Forest, Dartmoor, the Cotswolds and the Welsh countryside. Along the way they stopped in Oxford, where they visited Alice in Wonderland's shop and had fish and chips in a pub, huddled under an outdoor umbrella as it poured down with rain in the middle of summer. They went to football matches in London, Manchester and Cardiff, and despite not being a great fan of soccer, Marge couldn't help getting swept up in the atmosphere and camaraderie of such a world event. At each arena they chatted to people from several different countries, mostly with no particular allegiance to the competing teams, so the crowd was well behaved and cheered everyone on equally. They went to London as well, which hadn't changed much since she was there in the 80s, but the Millennium Eye was new and gave some splendid views over London, and they toured Buckingham Palace and then felt very posh when they went for afternoon tea at Claridge's hotel. As a special treat, Karleen took her to the Churchill War Museum, which was incorporated into the old underground Ministry of Defence rooms where Churchill and his government had led the war effort in the 1940s. Several rooms had been left exactly as they were when the staff and government ministers stood up and left in 1945, and Marge was especially fascinated to see the rooms where Churchill had worked and the provisions and notices scattered around on walls and shelves. As she wandered through the rooms she listened to his famous speeches being replayed on a speaker overhead, and it took her back to a time when she had first heard them, sitting around an old wireless with her mother and sisters in their old dining room in Horsham.

As she'd now been to England, Scotland and Wales, she wanted to see Ireland as well, so she booked a tour and flew over from London. She was nervous at first, as she'd never done a tour on her own before, but on the very first night she was invited by some of her companions to join them for dinner, and so she made friends and had company on the trip. She was fascinated by the country's history and landscape, so green and wild and different from England. She even tried some Guinness at the Guinness Storehouse, just as she had tried the whisky in Scotland, since she felt it would have been rude not to.

When she got home she was very pleased to be able to tell people she'd been to the Olympics, and several of her clubs and societies asked her to give a talk about it. A month later Norwood won the premiership again, the first one since 1997. The following year she and the family travelled up to the Sunshine Coast in Queensland for another Stevens reunion. Jess had died in 2010, but Pat, June and Colin were there, and she was able to visit Mary who was in hospital and would only live for a few months more.

Later in 2013 she took another trip to Europe, this time a cruise down the river Danube from Amsterdam to Budapest. She travelled with Chic and Guy again, and her niece Lois, and they had a leisurely but wonderful time, exploring pretty towns and villages during the days and watching the hills, castles and vineyards of Europe drift by from the boat in the evenings. In Amsterdam she was most struck by the museum of Anne Frank, which incorporates the small attic where she and her family had hidden during the war. They had a final stop in Prague, and she was home again in time for another Norwood premiership and the last ever game at Football Park.

In 2015, another opportunity came along, and this was a once-in-a-lifetime chance she couldn't pass up – a trip to Anzac Cove in Turkey for the 100-year anniversary of the Gallipoli landings. It was an invitation only service, and when one came her way, she wasn't about to say no.

Chapter Fourteen – The Things That Really Matter

Once again she travelled on her own, but it was an organised tour and the agency paired her with another lady, also travelling on her own, and so they looked out for each other. They arrived in Turkey a few days before the anniversary and were taken on many guided tours around the area, and to several war memorials including the Australian and American ones. They also explored the former battlefields, where they walked in the trenches where the troops had earned the nickname of the Diggers. It was a peaceful place – once a wasteland devoid of plants and littered with barbed wire and shrapnel, it was now quiet and sunny, with trees rustling gently in the breeze and the sound of the ocean lapping against the shore in the distance.

Marge found it fascinating to be there with a group, as there were many stories of relatives and ancestors who had fought there – including a tale from a 91-year-old man whose father had been killed on the shore as he made his way from the boat to the beach. The guide, with the help of a local historian, was able to identify the exact beach on which he had been shot. Several stories like this emerged in the days leading up to the anniversary, so that by the evening of April 24 each of them felt a deeper connection to the place and a sense of solidarity with their fellow travellers. They made their way to the site in stages, starting on the afternoon before the anniversary. Those who didn't have seats for the service and would be watching on a screen nearby had to leave first, but Marge had a ticket and so didn't need to be ready until midnight. She had a nap in the evening and then got dressed, warm clothes on against the cool of the night. Belatedly, she was informed that there would not be food provided and she would have to take her own, so she grabbed the only things that were within reach – six pieces of French stick, and two apples. They would have to do.

She was shown to her seat and sat down with one of her new friends, huddled in her beanie, scarf and rug. They sat through the night, chatting in the darkness as the hours ticked by, tired but full of anticipation and buoyed up by the feeling of excitement which rippled around the crowd. The air was cold, but they were warm under their blankets, and it didn't seem very long until the sky began getting lighter, and the sun could be seen lifting its head above the horizon. A hush descended over the crowd as the officials took their places, and the service began.

It was a surreal and remarkable moment, as she sat there in the crowd of more than 10,000 pilgrims and dignitaries, honoured to count herself among them for such a special and historic occasion. The Princes Charles and Harry were there and she could see them down at the front as well as on a big screen, as the service was read and the bugler played the Last Post, wavering on a note or two under the pressure of the occasion. They stood as the sun rose and light flooded the beach, reflecting off the water and making the trees around them glow golden yellow, and the various ministers and politicians recounted stories of the troops who had landed on the same shore a hundred years before. The Australian Prime Minister, Tony Abbot, gave a moving speech, describing the Anzacs as ordinary men who did extraordinary things, and so became the founding heroes of modern Australia. He talked about courage, love and sacrifice from both sides, and as the crowd intoned 'Lest We Forget', Marge couldn't help agreeing with him when he said: *'so much has changed in one hundred years, but not the things that really matter'.*

Once the formalities were over they were taken to another service at the Australian War Memorial, where Marge was disappointed not to be sitting in the front row as they all shook hands with Prince Harry, his red hair just visible to Marge a few rows back. Then it was a long wait for their bus to pick them up, as the many thousands of visitors tried to get back to their hotels and boats. She was extremely tired and hungry by now, her bread and apples long since consumed, but it was worth it – she knew how lucky she was to have been there, and that such an opportunity would never come up again.

She was still tired when she got home and her back was hurting her more than usual, but she didn't regret the trip and enjoyed an upsurge in popularity for a while as once again her groups and societies asked her to come and talk about her trip. She kept her travel ambitions more modest after that, and limited herself to visiting relatives, including her annual trip up to Brisbane. In 2016 she joined the family in Horsham for another reunion, and they enjoyed a very special day on a bus tour visiting the places where Jack and his siblings had grown up in Murtoa, and seeing the graves of Frederick and Katherine at the Murtoa cemetery and of Frederick's father William at the cemetery in Moyston. They finished the day with a visit to Sudholz Farm – the same one where Frederick, Jim, Jack and Ivan had worked many years ago, and still owned by the Sudholz family, who were kind enough to show their visitors around and give them a shearing demonstration. The next day they picnicked at Green Lake, just as Marge, Jack and their siblings had done in their youth. Jack's two remaining sisters Pat and June were there, and they talked proudly of their childhood, their parents and the places they'd known.

Later that year, Marge underwent surgery to relieve the pain in her back, which was, in her own words 'simply worn out', and had been troubling her for several years. The doctors suggested a new treatment from America in which two metal rods are inserted on either side of the spine and an electric charge blocks the nerves sending pain signals to the brain. The surgery was a success, and once the wounds healed she was able to stop taking pain medication entirely, for the first time in several years. The only thing she had to remember now was to charge the rods each day, which she did by holding an external power pack against a small internal one placed just under the skin on her buttocks. The grandchildren found it fascinating, of course, and started calling her 'Bionic Nanna', but for Marge it was an enormous relief, and though it didn't stop her from being tired, at least it meant she could keep doing the things she loved without being in constant pain.

In May 2017 she celebrated her 90th birthday, and this time she chose a masquerade theme, complete with music from all her favourite musicals. The family arranged to hire a hall this time (which meant it didn't rain, of course!) and Chic and Kaysie, with a small army of helpers, decorated it with masks, balloons and a lot of sparkly confetti. Once again there was food, drink and plenty of dancing, and Marge got into the spirit of things by dyeing her hair pink and wearing a pink glittery mask. So many of her friends were there – her old colleagues from John Martin's, her friend Vaughn from their days in Mildura, Jan and Thelma from the War Widows Guild, friends from her sewing group and even a couple she and Jack had met on their first trip to Europe. Her friend Joyce, who had spent so much time with Marge when she was first widowed, was not there, as she had passed away a few years before, but lots of family flew in, including Sue and Barry Jackson and a large contingent from Tasmania.

Marge was filled with pride as her children and grandchildren gave speeches and the great-grandchildren put on some dances to entertain everyone. From her vantage point up on the stage she looked out over a room full of all the people who meant the most to her, and who had stayed by her side through the ups and downs of her long and interesting life. Finally she looked at her children, her proudest achievement, who had all achieved their own success and happiness, and was filled with happiness for them. And as she looked back over the years, at the people who represented all the places she'd been and all the adventures she'd had, she realised that she was one of the lucky ones, and she knew, in that moment, that if she could do her life over again, she'd do it all exactly the same.

* * *

Postscript

There are a few more stories to tell, or rather, some loose strands to Marge's story that need to be tied up. The first is regarding Marge's father, Robert. After not seeing or hearing from him for five years, Kathleen made the decision to file for divorce in 1950. Via a solicitor, she attempted to make contact with him through the Central Army Records Office, but they would not disclose his whereabouts and so the divorce was never processed. That was the last anyone heard of him until more than twenty years later, when one of his granddaughters, Norma's daughter Georgina, began a new attempt to find him. She had no luck for several years, until finally she came across a death certificate and discovered that he had died from lung cancer on October 3, 1972 at Fairfield Hospital in Sydney, aged 68 years.

Finding the certificate brought up a lot of mixed feelings for the family, but the surprise that followed was an even greater one, for listed on the certificate were the names not of Marge and her siblings, but of six other children that Georgina didn't recognise. Kathleen's name was not on it, but another woman's was.

It didn't take very long for the family to determine what had happened. Robert had met another woman, probably when he was stationed in Queensland in the last few years of the war, and upon being discharged had returned to her, and not to Kathleen. He had also started using his middle name Walter, instead of Henry, which made him even more difficult to find.

When she received this information Marge was not altogether surprised, as she had suspected, when she was older and more inclined to think about it, that something like that must have happened. Nor were most of her newly discovered half-siblings, who had also suspected that their father must have had some secrets related to his life before he met their mother.

Once they'd had time to come to terms with this discovery, most of them were happy to meet up and so Marge has now met two of her half-brothers and a half-sister. Marge, naturally, was curious to know more about her father, but they could reveal nothing except that he had declined to attend any army functions or war reunions throughout his life. Certain details – such as the status of their parents' marriages – were not discussed, and Marge was just happy that she had a chance to get to know more family members. In her two new brothers, especially, she could see the family resemblance – one of them looked very much like Robert, and the other strongly resembled her brother Freddie.

Robert's death certificate has now been updated with all his children's names, as well as that of his first wife, Kathleen, and Marge still receives visits from time to time when her new family members pass through Adelaide.

The second matter relates to Marge's first daughter, the stillborn twin. Marge had never been to see the grave, something which had always bothered her, but which she'd been able to put out of her mind most of the time. Eventually, when she was approaching her 80th birthday, the niggle became too great and she went with her sister Bonny, who was still living in Horsham, to find the place where her daughter was buried. They found the spot, with the help of the cemetery attendant, but there was no headstone, or cross, or anything to mark the grave at all.

Marge made the decision there and then to do something about it, and Bonny helped her with the arrangements. When it came to choosing the inscription for the new headstone, she realised the child didn't have a name, and she appealed to her elder sister for advice.

"Well, what's your middle name?" Bonny asked her.

"Frances," Marge replied.

"Well then, that can be her name."

And so it was that Bonny named her first niece, and Frances Stevens' grave was finally marked with a headstone bearing her name and the date of November 4, 1948.

With her mind finally at ease over Frances' grave there was one final piece of unfinished business, and that was the fjords in Milford Sound. She and Jack had never made it back together, but Marge finally made it in January of 2018 when she went on a cruise with Kaysie, Chic and two of their friends around the North and South Islands of New Zealand. On the scheduled day they were up and out on their balcony by 5 a.m. to watch as the ship entered the majestic stretch of water, and they stayed out for several hours, quite content in their dressing gowns and slippers, sipping coffee as they watched mountains, waterfalls and the crystal-clear water of the Sound go past.

And so this story ends, although Marge's hasn't. She is still as busy as ever and involved in numerous clubs and societies. She loves to travel and visits Chic and Guy up in Brisbane every year, and the family in Victoria when she can. She is often to be found cheering on the Redlegs from the Stevens' box at Norwood Oval, and she still packs a thermos and sandwiches for everybody.

She still has the scar on her back, from when she had pneumonia at age five and the doctors did not expect her to live, although she's collected a few more scars since then. She still has the stool she made herself when she was pregnant with Ron and Frances, sitting in the small sitting room of the first home she shared with Jack. She still has the pearls that Jack gave her on their wedding day, when she felt like the prettiest girl who ever walked down an aisle. But most importantly, perhaps, she still has her optimism, her resilience and her ability to find joy in life, even in the difficult times and even when she was fighting for her life. In her early years she learned from her mother what it is to be cherished and comforted, and has spent the rest of her life passing it on. She seems to inherently know that love can never be divided, only multiplied, and therefore it can never run out. Perhaps this is how she inspires so many others, to keep trying, to keep smiling, and to keep searching for the joy in life. Of her many talents, perhaps this is her greatest one – fortunately, it's one she's always been happy to share.

In memory of

Yvonne 'Bonny' Dooling
1926 – 2021

Patricia 'Pat' Inglis
1932 – 2020

June Hallmond
1934 – 2022

Acknowledgments

Writing about my grandmother's life has been a tremendous honour and privilege, not to mention insightful and informative. I thought I knew her pretty well before I started, and have always admired her energy and optimism – now I realise that she is a stronger and more resilient woman that I could possibly have guessed.

As you may imagine, the process has also been a challenging one, and I could not have done it without a lot of help from a lot of people. And so, to the following I offer my heartfelt thanks and deepest gratitude:

Ron Stevens, Katherine Hamilton, Greg Stevens, Christine Nelson, Yvonne Preusker, Wayne Stevens, Robyn Gloede, Sharon Percy, Louis Stevens, June Hallmond, Pam Dettman, Louise Stevens, Lois Perrett, Jan Stevens and Belinda Stevens for their contributions to the family histories as well as their personal recollections, which have enriched the story considerably.

Courtney Goltz at the Australian War Memorial, Graham Gibson of the Rats of Tobruk Association, Jillian Hiscock of the Royal Historical Society of Victoria, Catherine Manning of the History Trust of South Australia, Hannah Bourne from Scouts SA, Moira Drew of the Australian Red Cross, Kent Watson of Monument Australia, Bridget Penna and her colleague Haylee, for their invaluable information and fact checking assistance.

Mary Mitchell-Gogay and Debbie Morgan for their proof-reading prowess, and all my beta-readers for their feedback and encouragement.

Graeme Whittle for the wonderful cover image, and Ben Stevens for the book and cover design.

My dad, Greg Stevens, for believing that I could pull this off, and supporting me through the whole process – including making a lot of inquiries on my behalf, responding to my dozens of emails and a lot of general reassurance.

Pat Inglis, who contributed to this story though she isn't here to see the final product. I hope you would have liked it Aunty Pat.

And finally to my nanna, Marge, for allowing me to write this story, for sitting through several hours of interviews and sharing your memories of times both good and bad, and for waiting so patiently for the result. I hope I've done your story justice, and, while I hope I haven't allowed too much bias to creep in, that readers of this tale will understand just how amazing you are. I know that you continue so inspire so many people, not just to live life to its fullest, but to be kind and patient, to love without prejudice, to support without judgement and to give without expectation or agenda. Thank you, most of all, for being you, and know that I am, and always will be, proud to be your granddaughter.

* * *

Bibliography

Abelson, Peter & Chung, Demi, Housing Prices in Australia: 1970 to 2003. Accessed online at http://www.econ.mq.edu.au/__data/assets/pdf_file/0018/220581/Abelson_9_04.pdf

Australian Broadcasting Corporation website, accessed online at https://about.abc.net.au/abc-history/

Australianfootball.com, accessed online at https://australianfootball.com

The Australian Food History Timeline, accessed online at https://australianfoodtimeline.com.au

Biography of John Fairlie Forrest, The Geelong College, accessed online at https://gnet.geelongcollege.vic.edu.au/wiki/FORREST-Rev-John-Fairlie-1901-1971.ashx

Currency conversions and rates calculated by The Reserve Bank of Australia Pre-Decimal Inflation Calculator, accessed online at https://www.rba.gov.au/calculator/annualPreDecimal.html

Discover Murray River website, accessed online at http://www.murrayriver.com.au/about-the-murray/1956-murray-river-floods/

History of the Norwood Football Club, accessed online at http://www.redlegsmuseum.com.au HOME.aspx

Lovemoney.com, accessed online at https://www.lovemoney.com/gallerylist/62942/the-bestselling-products-of-the-60s-how-many-do-you-remember

Ruffalo, Mark, A Brief History of Electroconvulsive Therapy, accessed online at https://www.psychologytoday.com/gb/blog/freud-fluoxetine/201811/brief-history-electroconvulsive-therapy

Russo, Naomi, Now and Then: Australia's 'six o'clock swill'. 8 February 2016, Australian Geographic. Accessed online at https://www.australiangeographic.com.au/topics/history-culture/2016/02/now-and-then-australias-six-oclock-swill/

Tarbotton, David, Celebrating 80 Years Since the Empire Games, 4 February 2018, Sydney Cricket Ground. Accessed online at https://www.scgt.nsw.gov.au/whats-on/latest-news/celebrating-80-years-since-the-empire-games/

Television.AU, accessed online at https://televisionau.com/

The Australian Commonwealth Games official website, accessed online at https://commonwealthgames.com.au/1938-british-empire-games-opens-in-sydney/

The Commonwealth Games Federation website, accessed online at https://thecgf.com/games/sydney-1938

The Crows History Locker, accessed online at *https://crowshistory.afc.com.au/*

The AFL official website, accessed online at *https://www.afl.com.au/*

Van Raay, Lara, Memories of the Queen: the 1954 Royal Visit, from ABC Open Sunraysia, 20 October 2011. Accessed online at *https://www.abc.net.au/local/stories/2011/10/20/3344618.htm*

Newspaper articles

150, from The Riverine Grazier, Friday 28 January 1938, page 2. Accessed online at *https://trove.nla.gov.au/newspaper/article/137357143?searchTerm=sydney%20150%20year%20celebrations*

Australian Day of Rejoicing, from The Sydney Morning Herald, Thursday 27 January 1938, page 11. Accessed online at *https://trove.nla.gov.au/newspaper/article/17443998?searchTerm=sydney%20150%20year%20celebrations*

Boy Dies in Bale of Wool, from The Newcastle Morning Herald and Miners' Advocate, Saturday 6 September 1952, page 1. Accessed online at *https://trove.nla.gov.au/newspaper/article/133564288?searchTerm=child%20dies%20in%20wool%20presser*

Congratulations, from The Sydney Morning Herald, Friday 4 February 1938, page 12. Accessed online at *https://trove.nla.gov.au/newspaper/article/17427419?searchTerm=sydney%20150%20year%20celebrations*

Dedication of Miniature Shrine Model, from The Horsham Times, Tuesday 5 December 1944, page 2. Accessed online at *https://trove.nla.gov.au/newspaper/article/72717456?searchTerm=horsham%20war%20dead%20horsham%20war%20casualties%20honour%20roll%20statistics*

Governor Opens 150 Show, from the Horsham Times, Friday 6 October 1950, Page 1. Accessed online at *https://trove.nla.gov.au/newspaper/page/7071775*

Horsham Honours War Dead, from The Horsham Times, Tuesday 14 November 1944, page 2. Accessed online at *https://trove.nla.gov.au/newspaper/article/72717113?searchTerm=horsham%20war%20dead%20horsham%20war%20casualties%20honour%20roll%20statistics*

Queen's Memorable Flying Visit to Mildura, from The Age, Friday 26 March 1954, page 1. Accessed online at *https://trove.nla.gov.au/newspaper/article/205707324?searchTerm=queen%27s%20visit%20to%20mildura*

Red Cross Emergency Company Disbanded, from The Horsham Times, Friday 10 May 1946, page 2. Accessed online at *https://trove.nla.gov.au/newspaper/article/73077176?searchTerm=horsham%20red%20cross%20train%20railway%20station*

Royal Visit to Mildura, from The Chronicle, Thursday 1 April 1954, page 48. Accessed online at *https://trove.nla.gov.au/newspaper/article/93943852?searchTerm=queen%27s%20visit%20to%20mildura*

The Schools, from The Sydney Morning Herald, Thursday 10 June 1937, page 5. Accessed online at *https://trove.nla.gov.au/newspaper/article/17374592?searchTerm=sydney%20150%20year%20celebrations*

Wild Excitement as Horsham Celebrates Victory, from The Horsham Times, Friday 17 August 1945, page 2. Accessed online at *https://trove.nla.gov.au/newspaper/article/73174593?searchTerm=victory%2C%20surrender%2C%20war*

Military History

Australian War Memorial Collection, accessed online at *https://www.awm.gov.au/*

Fascinating Historical Facts - Mornington Peninsula - Balcombe Army Camp - Balcombe Estuary Mount Martha, Discover Mornington Peninsula. Accessed online at *http://www.discovermorningtonpeninsula.com.au/fascinatingfacts/balcombe-estuary.php*

Gladwin, Michael, Captains of the Soul. Big Sky Publishing, Australia, 2013.

Jones, JJ, Balcombe Army Camp – Mount Martha. 1 April 2009, Mornington Peninsula. Accessed online at *https://ezinearticles.com/?Balcombe-Army-Camp---Mount-Martha---Historical-Facts,-Mornington-Peninsula,-Victoria&id=2172478*

Recollections of Tobruk from an interview with Fr Cyril Francis, interviewed by Martin Hadlow 16 April 1979, accessed via Australian War Memorial Research Centre.

Records of the 2/13th Australian Infantry Battalion, accessed online at *https://www.awm.gov.au/collection/U56056*

The Horsham War Memorial, from Monument Australia, accessed online at *https://monumentaustralia.org.au/themes/conflict/multiple/display/94701-horsham-and-district-war-memorial-and-cenotaph*

The National Archives of Australia, including information on the Vietnam conscription lottery, accessed online at *https://www.naa.gov.au/*

WW2 Unit diaries of the 2/13th Infantry Battalion, accessed online at *https://www.awm.gov.au/ collection/C1361029*

WW2 Unit Diaries of the 7th Australian Infantry Battalion, accessed online at *https://www.awm.gov.au/collection/C1361025*

About the Author

Karleen Stevens was born and grew up in Adelaide, Australia. She trained as a journalist at the University of South Australia and began her writing career at a newspaper in the Barossa Valley before travelling to Europe to pursue her other great passion, travel. She now lives and works in West Sussex in the UK where she documents her adventures at karleenstevens.blog. In The Mood is her first published biography.

Website: *https://karleenstevens.journoportfolio.com/*

LI: *https://www.linkedin.com/in/karleen-stevens-freelance-writer-travel-events-hospitality-sustainability/*

fb: *https://www.facebook.com/karleenstevensblogger*

ig: *@karleenstevensblogger*

www.ingramcontent.com/pod-product-compliance
Lightning Source LLC
Chambersburg PA
CBHW010245010526
44107CB00063B/2686